FRIEDMAN & SZASZ
ON LIBERTY AND DRUGS

FRIEDMAN & SZASZ ON LIBERTY AND DRUGS

ESSAYS ON THE FREE MARKET AND PROHIBITION

Edited and with a Preface by
Arnold S. Trebach and Kevin B. Zeese

THE DRUG POLICY FOUNDATION PRESS · Washington, D.C.

THE DRUG POLICY FOUNDATION PRESS
4455 Connecticut Ave., N.W., Suite B500
Washington, D.C. 20008
Phone: (202) 895-1634
Fax: (202) 537-3007

First printing 1992
Printed and bound in the United States of America

Excerpts and notes from Chapter 7 in *Free to Choose: A Personal Statement*, copyright © 1980 by Milton Friedman and Rose D. Friedman, reprinted by permission of Harcourt Brace Jovanovich, Inc. • Chapter 7 from *Tyranny of the Status Quo*, copyright © 1984 by Milton Friedman and Rose D. Friedman, reprinted by permission of Harcourt Brace Jovanovich, Inc. • Table 1 from *Ceremonial Chemistry: The Ritual Persecution of Drugs, Addicts, and Pushers* is reprinted with the permission of Learning Publications, Inc. Copyright 1985 by Thomas S. Szasz. All rights reserved

Library of Congress Catalog Card Number: 92-073701
ISBN: 1-879189-05-4

The Drug Policy Foundation is a charitable corporation under the laws of the District of Columbia and a tax-exempt, public foundation under section 501(c)(3) of the U.S. Internal Revenue Code. The Drug Policy Foundation neither seeks nor accepts government funding. Contributions to the Foundation are tax deductible.

The error of supposing that the behavior of social organisms can be shaped at will is widespread. It is the fundamental error of most so-called reformers. It explains why they so often feel that the fault lies in the man, not the "system"; that the way to solve problems is to "turn the rascals out" and put well-meaning people in charge. It explains why their reforms, when ostensibly achieved, so often go astray.

—*Milton Friedman*

After generations of living under medical tutelage, which provides us with protection (albeit illusory) against "dangerous drugs," we have failed to cultivate the self-reliance and self-discipline we must possess as competent adults surrounded by the fruits of our pharmacological-technological age.

—*Thomas S. Szasz*

Contents

Preface

Arnold S. Trebach and Kevin B. Zeese

> Nothing in this world is more important than personal liberty.
> Many people are in favor of blotting out the sun to prevent the
> growth of weeds. This is the mistake of all prohibitory fanaticism.
> —Robert G. Ingersoll (1833–1899)

Milton Friedman and Thomas Szasz are old-fashioned liberals. Essentially, they believe in inalienable individual rights and in sharply limited government powers, as originally set forth in the U.S. Constitution. Friedman and Szasz oppose much that modern liberals value, such as the welfare state, government control of businesses and the professions, and the restrictive regulation of drugs. But they believe that a society founded on individual liberty must oppose pervasive government control because the powers of government ultimately rest on coercion.

Thus, both of these scholars fit within the modern movement labeled "libertarian." Indeed, both have reached the status of icons or cult heroes in libertarian circles. Yet, their celebrity goes far beyond libertarians. Both are viewed as among the great minds of the century in their respective fields—Friedman in economics and Szasz in psychiatry. Both have won great respect from thinking people across the political spectrum.

Both also have their harsh critics who claim that Friedman and Szasz do not understand the benefits that flow from social welfare programs and the government restraint of big businesses. Liberty, say the critics, is not our society's paramount virtue, particularly for the poor and the handicapped. Some, including supporters of the Drug Policy Foundation, have charged, for example, that Friedman was partly responsible for the disregard of the poor under Reagan; while others have charged that Szasz's criticisms of treatment programs have hindered many forms of outreach to the mentally ill and the addicted.

Although this anthology is focused principally on drug policy, we hope that readers will see the larger tapestry from which their drug arguments are cut. Drug policy reform has major implications for what one believes about society and human nature. For example, the touchy issue of suicide is, in some ways, anterior to the issue of drug use. What one says about suicide indicates the weight that one gives to self-control and personal responsibility.

Because both Friedman and Szasz are brilliant writers with sparse styles, they present their views with a clarity and directness that defies conventional rhetoric. This attribute makes them all the more appealing to those who agree with them and has quite the contrary effect on their detractors. For readers of any persuasion, however, it is a pleasure to be in the company of such good writers.

Their views on drugs, like their views on many other matters, are out on the farthest frontiers of policy reform. Many drug policy reformers have spent years fashioning mid-level compromises that would decriminalize only a few drugs, while leaving the engine of prohibition intact and running. Not so with Friedman and Szasz. They advocate repealing prohibition with its harsh ethos of criminal sanctions and, in its place, leaving a thoroughly new system powered by the free market and a belief in the primacy of individual choice.

It is clear that Friedman and Szasz are true radicals. As Friedman notes in *Capitalism and Freedom,* there are two senses to the word radical.[1] We want to stress here the sense that means "root" (the word *radical* is derived from the Latin word for root, *radix*). In drug policy, as in other fields, both Friedman and Szasz address the root of the matter: Where do government coercion and individual liberty intersect? Both men side with individual liberty because its principles are fundamental to the foundation of our country.

It is worth noting that neither Friedman nor Szasz is an anarchist. Both men agree that our government's primary duties include (1) defending the coasts and (2) providing and maintaining a criminal justice system. They extrapolate from these clear-cut duties that our government is barred from intervening in the voluntary, peaceful activities of adults—a view that the Founding Fathers deeply respected after decades of insensitive and harsh rule by an overseas government.

Although Friedman and Szasz proceed from similar principles, we have juxtaposed their arguments in this book because both men craft their arguments from widely different points of view. Friedman argues principally from statistics and the standpoint of the market;* whereas, Szasz discusses moral principles and the effects of scapegoating on human laws and language. A brief overview of each writer is in order.

Friedman has consistently pointed out that, while the drug warriors have fixated chiefly on statistics about the *levels* of drug use, other statistics—about rates of homicides, rates of violent crimes, and prison populations, for example—have been increasing dramatically as the drug war has been intensified. The result is a less orderly society, to put it mildly. To be sure, drug warriors use the rising crime rates to create self-fulfilling justifications for more and harsher anti-drug laws. Friedman does not think that this maneuver follows, because, according to his reasoning, there is an indisputable connection between prohibition and crime. Friedman proposes that we repeal prohibition—a move that would not repeal *caveat emptor*—and deal with drugs on the clean slate of reason.

Friedman acknowledges that the repeal of drug prohibition will change the levels of demand for certain drugs, but he does not believe that drug use will necessarily increase, particularly over the long run. The difficulty with such a prediction lies in comparing the demand for legal drugs with the demand for illegal drugs. Friedman believes, for instance, that the high demand for crack cocaine will not survive drug prohibition. People act in their own best interests, insists Friedman, and it is hard to imagine people rejecting decades of anti-drug rhetoric to embrace a highly potent form of cocaine when other, more healthful options exist.

As distinguished from Friedman's cost-benefit analyses, Szasz builds his arguments on the U.S. government's lack of constitutional authority to impose healthful habits on its citizens. While many Americans agree that the government should not regulate a people's habits, Szasz points out that our language has been warped to circumvent the soundness of this statement. Hence, it is commonly reported that many crimes are caused by an illegal drug, not by a person. The animation of inert (illegal) chemicals is directly related to the need to subvert or deny personal responsibility. And personal responsibility is anathema to a war *on drugs*.

But see Prof. Friedman's comments about the role of economics in morality in Chapter 8, "On Liberty and Drugs," page 71.

One example of the decay of language is the universal and un-qualified acceptance of the idea that certain, unpopular behaviors are "diseases" that can be corrected by "treatment" or, more perniciously, by "compulsory treatment." Szasz argues that the corruption of language "convinces" people that objective solutions exist for subjective problems. Szasz contends that, instead of people's recognizing that free will sometimes has unpleasant consequences, our language envelopes us in the promises of more comfortable beliefs. Szasz describes this predicament elsewhere as part of an "institutionalized denial of the tragic nature of life...."[2] In the tradition of George Orwell, Szasz opts for the honest use of language as the means for clear thinking about drug policy.

Friedman's and Szasz's arguments bring drug policy to its ulti-mate resting place for the classical liberal: drugs are property that all adults are entitled to possess, manufacture, consume, and sell like any other consumer goods—responsibly. This argument is a new frame-work for drug policy, but it is as old as the philosophical underpin-nings of our nation. For example, a brief look at the Ninth Amend-ment illustrates the deep currents of classical liberalism in our nation's heritage.

The ratification of the new Constitution depended upon Con-gress's guaranteeing the protection of certain rights under the new federal government. The Federalists opposed any sort of bill of rights because it was redundant—the Constitution delegated specific powers; it did not take away any more rights than was necessary for the gov-ernment to perform its duties.[3] Although a Federalist, James Madison supported amending the Constitution with a bill of rights, as long as those amendments included the following condition:

> The exceptions here or elsewhere in the constitution, made in favor of particular rights, shall not be so construed as to diminish the just importance of other rights retained by the people, or as to enlarge the powers delegated by the constitution; but either as actual limitations of such powers, or as inserted merely for greater caution.[4]

For Madison, then, the most powerful argument against a bill of rights was that, "by enumerating particular exceptions to the [federal gov-ernment's] grant of power, it [a bill of rights] would *disparage* those rights which were not placed in that enumeration…."[5] Madison wanted it to be clear that a bill of rights would not and could not be an exhaustive list.

What was obvious to many of the Framers—the fact that, in Jefferson's words, "the purposes of society do not require a surrender of all our rights to our ordinary governors"—was distilled into the Ninth Amendment, which is a reminder that the government is made up of only selected powers over individual liberty.[6]

The Framers believed that individual rights were not man-made or conferred by the government. Rather they were part of each human being's natural birthright. That is precisely what Jefferson meant when he wrote that people have "unalienable rights," which are secured, not established, by democratic governments. The government, then, is left with the duty of securing individual rights within the scope of its powers.

The view that the individual has certain rights to make choices in everyday life has been one enunciated throughout the history of the United States. In 1849, Henry David Thoreau wrote in *Civil Disobedience* that "there will never be a really free and enlightened State until the State comes to recognize the individual as a higher and independent power, from which all its own power and authority are derived…."

During the twentieth century, Justice Louis Brandeis framed this point with reference to the Bill of Rights as a whole and the Ninth Amendment in particular in *Olmstead v. United States:*

> The makers of our Constitution undertook to secure conditions favorable to the pursuit of happiness. They recognized the significance of man's spiritual nature, of his feelings, and of his intellect. They knew that only a part of the pain, pleasure, and satisfaction of life are to be found in material things. They sought to protect Americans in their beliefs, their thoughts, their emotions, and their sensations. They conferred, as against the government, the right to be let alone—the most comprehensive of rights and the right most valued by civilized men.[7]

While those views have dominated much of the American experience, there have always been countervailing views. One of these views is that people should not (or cannot) choose for themselves in certain areas of their lives.[8] Drug policy is an extreme example of how these views are crystallized into law.

We hope that this anthology will demonstrate how Friedman and Szasz respond to the growing faith in the "benevolence" of a big government. Our society's dictates about drug policy (or absence thereof) reflect the degree to which we rely on our nation's heritage of individual liberty and self-determination. The American experiment in liberty, as conceived by Jefferson, Madison, and other Revolutionaries, hangs in the balance.

Notes

[1] Milton Friedman, *Capitalism and Freedom* (Chicago: The University of Chicago Press, 1962, 1982), p. 6.

[2] Thomas Szasz, "Diagnoses are not diseases," *The Lancet*, vol. 338, p. 1574 (Dec. 21/28, 1991).

[3] For example, George Washington wrote to Lafayette that the American people gave to the new federal government only "a part of their original power in what manner and what proportion they think fit. They never part with the whole; and they retain the right of recalling what they part with.... To every suggestion concerning a bill of rights, the citizens of the United States may always say, 'We reserve the right to do what we please.'" 2 J. Elliot, *Debates in the Several State Conventions on the Adoption of the Federal Constitution* (2d edition, 1876), p. 437; *quoted in* Raoul Berger, "The Ninth Amendment," in *The Rights Retained by the People: The History and Meaning of the Ninth Amendment*, Randy E. Barnett, ed. (Fairfax, VA: George Mason University Press, 1989), p. 196 n.39.

[4] James Madison, "Speech to the House Explaining his Proposed Amendments and his Notes for the Amendment Speech," reprinted in Barnett, *The Rights Retained by the People*, p. 55.

[5] Ibid., p. 60 (emphasis added).

[6] The Ninth Amendment reads: "The enumeration in the Constitution of certain rights shall not be construed to deny or disparage others retained by the people."

[7] 277 U.S. 438, 478 (1928) (dissent).

[8] Witness former drug czar William Bennett's assertion "that government has a responsibility to craft and uphold laws that help educate citizens about right and wrong." William J. Bennett, "A Response to Milton Friedman," *The Wall Street Journal*, Sept. 19, 1989.

Acknowledgments

This book developed out of the Drug Policy Foundation's annual achievement awards. In 1991, the Foundation awarded Professor Friedman the Richard J. Dennis Drugpeace Award for Outstanding Achievement in the Field of Drug Policy Reform, and it awarded Dr. Szasz the Alfred R. Lindesmith Award for Achievement in the Field of Scholarship and Writing. During the Fifth Annual International Conference for Drug Policy Reform, Friedman and Szasz each gave a major speech and taped a half-hour interview for "America's Drug Forum."

Progress on the book began in and was sustained by the Foundation's Press Office. One of the Foundation's newest members, Rob Stewart, a closet libertarian, organized and edited the various articles and chapters down to a manageable whole. He also negotiated with publishers, printers, software dealers, and many others to produce the book. Kennington Wall and Dave Fratello assisted with the layout and the editing of the book. They also took turns playing devil's advocate on the selection of writings and the style. Karen Gusman, Meredith Feldman, Stacie Norton, and David Grinnell ensured the high fidelity of the reprinted material by painstakingly reviewing the text.

The staff of "America's Drug Forum"—Niki Mitchell, Stuart Suggs, and Patricia Westwater—deserve thanks for arranging and producing two exclusive interviews with Mssrs. Friedman and Szasz.

We wish also to thank Carolyn Shulman, Pamela Griffin, Karen, and Stacie who orchestrated the 1991 International Conference on Drug Policy Reform.

Finally, we wish to acknowledge the moral and financial support of Richard Dennis. Rich is an ardent supporter of libertarian thought. In addition, Rich made our annual achievement awards possible through an earmarked grant from the Chicago Resource Center. The Foundation would truly be a different place without him.

ARNOLD S. TREBACH
KEVIN B. ZEESE
Washington, D.C.

Part One

Milton Friedman

Chapter One

An Open Letter
to Bill Bennett*

Dear Bill:
 In Oliver Cromwell's eloquent words, "I beseech you, in
 the bowels of Christ, think it possible you may be mistaken"
about the course you and President Bush urge us to adopt to fight
drugs. The path you propose of more police, more jails, use of the
military in foreign countries, harsh penalties for drug users, and a
whole panoply of repressive measures can only make a bad situation
worse. The drug war cannot be won by those tactics without under-
mining the human liberty and individual freedom that you and I cher-
ish.

 You are not mistaken in believing that drugs are a scourge that is
devastating our society. You are not mistaken in believing that drugs
are tearing asunder our social fabric, ruining the lives of many young
people, and imposing heavy costs on some of the most disadvantaged
among us. You are not mistaken in believing that the majority of the
public share your concerns. In short, you are not mistaken in the end
you seek to achieve.

 Your mistake is failing to recognize that the very measures you
favor are a major source of the evils you deplore. Of course the problem is demand, but it is not only demand, it is demand that must
operate through repressed and illegal channels. Illegality creates ob-
scene profits that finance the murderous tactics of the drug lords;
illegality leads to the corruption of law enforcement officials; illegality
monopolizes the efforts of honest law forces so that they are starved

*William J. Bennett served as the Director of the White House's Office of
National Drug Control Policy from March 1989 to Nov. 1990.

for resources to fight the simpler crimes of robbery, theft, and assault.

Drugs are a tragedy for addicts. But criminalizing their use converts that tragedy into a disaster for society, for users and non-users alike. Our experience with the prohibition of drugs is a replay of our experience with the prohibition of alcoholic beverages.

I append excerpts from a column* that I wrote in 1972 on "Prohibition and Drugs." The major problem then was heroin from Marseilles; today, it is cocaine from Latin America. Today, also, the problem is far more serious than it was seventeen years ago: more addicts, more innocent victims; more drug pushers, more law enforcement officials; more money spent to enforce prohibition, more money spent to circumvent prohibition.

Had drugs been decriminalized seventeen years ago, "crack" would never have been invented (it was invented because the high cost of illegal drugs made it profitable to provide a cheaper version) and there would today be far fewer addicts. The lives of thousands, perhaps hundreds of thousands of innocent victims would have been saved, and not only in the United States. The ghettos of our major cities would not be drug-and-crime-infested no-man's lands. Fewer people would be in jails, and fewer jails would have been built.

Colombia, Bolivia, and Peru would not be suffering from narco-terror, and we would not be distorting our foreign policy because of narco-terror. Hell would not, in the words with which Billy Sunday welcomed Prohibition, "be forever for rent," but it would be a lot emptier.

Decriminalizing drugs is even more urgent now than in 1972, but we must recognize that the harm done in the interim cannot be wiped out, certainly not immediately. Postponing decriminalization will only make matters worse, and make the problem appear even more intractable.

Alcohol and tobacco cause many more deaths in users than do [illegal] drugs. Decriminalization would not prevent us from treating drugs as we now treat alcohol and tobacco: prohibiting sales of drugs to minors, outlawing the advertising of drugs, and similar measures. Such measures could be enforced, while outright prohibition cannot be. Moreover, if even a small fraction of the money we now spend on trying to enforce drug prohibition were devoted to treatment and

---

*See Chapter 5, "Crime," pages 39–43 for a version of this column.

rehabilitation, in an atmosphere of compassion not punishment, the reduction in drug usage and in the harm done to the users could be dramatic.

This plea comes from the bottom of my heart. Every friend of freedom, and I know you are one, must be as revolted as I am by the prospect of turning the United States into an armed camp, by the vision of jails filled with casual drug users and of an army of enforcers empowered to invade the liberty of citizens on slight evidence. A country in which shooting down unidentified planes "on suspicion" can be seriously considered as a drug war tactic is not the kind of United States that either you or I want to hand on to future generations.

MILTON FRIEDMAN

Chapter Two

The Role of Government in a Free Society

A common objection to totalitarian societies is that they regard the end as justifying the means. Taken literally, this objection is clearly illogical. If the end does not justify the means, what does? But this easy answer does not dispose of the objection; it simply shows that the objection is not well put. To deny that the end justifies the means is indirectly to assert that the end in question is not the ultimate end, that the ultimate end is itself the use of the proper means. Desirable or not, any end that can be attained only by the use of bad means must give way to the more basic end of the use of acceptable means.

To the liberal, the appropriate means are free discussion and voluntary cooperation, which implies that any form of coercion is inappropriate. The ideal is unanimity among responsible individuals achieved on the basis of free and full discussion. ...

From this standpoint, the role of the market ... is that it permits unanimity without conformity; that it is a system of effectively proportional representation. On the other hand, the characteristic feature of action through explicitly political channels is that it tends to require or to enforce substantial conformity. The typical issue must be decided "yes" or "no"; at most, provision can be made for a fairly limited number of alternatives. Even the use of proportional representation in its explicitly political form does not alter this conclusion. The number of separate groups that can in fact be represented is narrowly limited, enormously so by comparison with the proportional representation of the market. More important, the fact that the final outcome generally must be a law applicable to all groups, rather than separate legislative enactments for each "party" represented, means that proportional representation in its political version, far from permitting unanimity without conformity, tends toward ineffectiveness and fragmentation. It thereby operates to destroy any consensus on which unanimity with conformity can rest.

There are clearly some matters with respect to which effective proportional representation is impossible. I cannot get the amount of national defense I want and you, a different amount. With respect to such indivisible matters we can discuss, and argue, and vote. But having decided, we must conform. It is precisely the existence of such indivisible matters—protection of the individual and the nation from coercion are clearly the most basic—that prevents exclusive reliance on individual action through the market. If we are to use some of our resources for such indivisible items, we must employ political channels to reconcile differences.

The use of political channels, while inevitable, tends to strain the social cohesion essential for a stable society. The strain is least if agreement for joint action need be reached only on a limited range of issues on which people in any event have common views. Every extension of the range of issues for which explicit agreement is sought strains further the delicate threads that hold society together. If it goes so far as to touch an issue on which men feel deeply yet differently, it may well disrupt the society. Fundamental differences in basic values can seldom if ever be resolved at the ballot box; ultimately they can only be decided, though not resolved, by conflict. The religious and civil wars of history are a bloody testament to this judgment.

The widespread use of the market reduces the strain on the social fabric by rendering conformity unnecessary with respect to any activities it encompasses. The wider the range of activities covered by the market, the fewer are the issues on which explicitly political decisions are required and hence on which it is necessary to achieve agreement. In turn, the fewer the issues on which agreement is necessary, the greater is the likelihood of getting agreement while maintaining a free society.

Unanimity is, of course, an ideal. In practice, we can afford neither the time nor the effort that would be required to achieve complete unanimity on every issue. We must perforce accept something less. We are thus led to accept majority rule in one form or another as an expedient. That majority rule is an expedient rather than itself a basic principle is clearly shown by the fact that our willingness to resort to majority rule, and the size of the majority we require, themselves depend on the seriousness of the issue involved. If the matter is of little moment and the minority has no strong feelings about being overruled, a bare plurality will suffice. On the other hand, if the minority feels strongly about the issue involved, even a bare majority will not do. Few of us would be willing to have issues of free speech, for example, decided by a bare majority. Our legal structure is full of such distinctions among kinds of issues that require different kinds of majorities. At the extreme are those issues embodied in the Constitution. These are the principles that are so important that we are willing to make minimal concessions to expediency. Something like essential consensus was achieved initially in accepting them, and we require something like essential consensus for a change in them.

The self-denying ordinance to refrain from majority rule on certain kinds of issues that is embodied in our Constitution and in similar written or unwritten constitutions elsewhere, and the specific provisions in these constitutions or their equivalents prohibiting coercion of individuals, are themselves to be regarded as reached by free discussion and as reflecting essential unanimity about means.

I turn now to consider more specifically, though still in very broad terms, what the areas are that cannot be handled through the market at all, or can be handled only at so great a cost that the use of political channels may be preferable.

Government as Rulemaker and Umpire

It is important to distinguish the day-to-day activities of people from the general customary and legal framework within which these take place. The day-to-day activities are like the actions of the participants in a game when they are playing it; the framework, like the rules of the game they play. And just as a good game requires acceptance by the players both of the rules and of the umpire to interpret and enforce them, so a good society requires that its members agree on the general conditions that will govern relations among them, on some means of arbitrating different interpretations of these conditions, and on some device for enforcing compliance with the generally accepted rules. As in games, so also in society, most of the general conditions are the unintended outcome of custom, accepted unthinkingly. At most, we consider explicitly only minor modifications in them, though the cumulative effect of a series of minor modifications may be a drastic alteration in the character of the game or of the society. In both games and society also, no set of rules can prevail unless most participants most of the time conform to them without external sanctions; unless that is, there is a broad underlying social consensus. But we cannot rely on custom or on this consensus alone to interpret and to enforce the rules; we need an umpire. These then are the basic roles of government in a free society: to provide a means whereby we can modify the rules, to mediate differences among us on the meaning of the rules, and to enforce compliance with the rules on the part of those few who would otherwise not play the game.

The need for government in these respects arises because absolute freedom is impossible. However attractive anarchy may be as a philosophy, it is not feasible in a world of imperfect men. Men's freedoms can conflict, and when they do, one man's freedom must be limited to preserve another's—as a Supreme Court Justice once put it, "My freedom to move my fist must be limited by the proximity of your chin."

The major problem in deciding the appropriate activities of government is how to resolve such conflicts among the freedoms of different individuals. In some cases, the answer is easy. There is little difficulty in attaining near unanimity to the proposition that one man's freedom to murder his neighbor must be sacrificed to preserve the freedom of the other man to live. In other cases, the answer is difficult. In the economic area, a major problem arises in respect of the conflict between freedom to combine and freedom to compete. What meaning is to be attributed to *free* as modifying *enterprise?* In the United States, *free* has been understood to mean that anyone is free to set up an enterprise, which means that existing enterprises are not free to keep out competitors except by selling a better product at the same price or the same product at a lower price. In the continental tradition, on the other hand, the meaning has generally been that enterprises are free to do what they want, including the fixing of prices, division of markets, and the adoption of other techniques to keep out potential competitors. Perhaps the most difficult specific problem in this area arises with respect to combinations among laborers, where the problem of freedom to combine and freedom to compete is particularly acute.

A still more basic economic area in which the answer is both difficult and important is the definition of property rights. The notion of property, as it has developed over centuries and as it is embodied in our legal codes, has become so much a part of us that we tend to take it for granted, and fail to recognize the extent to which just what constitutes property and what rights the ownership of property confers are complex social creations rather than self-evident propositions. Does my having title to land, for example, and my freedom to use my property as I wish, permit me to deny to someone else the right to fly over my land in his airplane? Or does his right to use his airplane take precedence? Or does this depend on how high he flies? Or how much noise he makes? Does voluntary exchange require that he pay me for the privilege of flying over my land? Or that I must pay him to refrain from flying over it? The mere mention of royalties, copyrights, patents; shares of stock in corporations; riparian rights, and the like, may perhaps emphasize the role of generally accepted social rules in the very definition of property. It may suggest also that, in many cases, the existence of a well specified and generally accepted definition of property is far more important than just what the definition is.

Another economic area that raises particularly difficult problems is the monetary system. Government responsibility for the monetary system has long been recognized. It is explicitly provided for in the constitutional provision which gives Congress the power "to coin money, regulate the value thereof, and of foreign coin." There is probably no other area of economic activity with respect to which government action has been so uniformly accepted. This habitual and by now almost unthinking acceptance of governmental responsibility makes thorough understanding of the grounds for such responsibility all the more necessary, since it enhances the danger that the scope of government will spread from activities that are, to those that are not, appropriate in a free society, from providing a monetary framework to determining the allocation of resources among individuals. ...

In summary, the organization of economic activity through voluntary exchange presumes that we have provided, through government, for the maintenance of law and order to prevent coercion of one individual by another, the enforcement of contracts voluntarily entered into, the definition of the meaning of property rights, the interpretation and enforcement of such rights, and the provision of a monetary framework. ...

Action through Government on Paternalistic Grounds

Freedom is a tenable objective only for responsible individuals. We do not believe in freedom for madmen or children. The necessity of drawing a line between responsible individuals and others is inescapable, yet it means that there is an essential ambiguity in our ultimate objective of freedom. Paternalism is inescapable for those whom we designate as not responsible.

The clearest case, perhaps, is that of madmen. We are willing neither to permit them freedom nor to shoot them. It would be nice if we could rely on voluntary activities of individuals to house and care for the madmen. But I think we cannot rule out the possibility that such charitable activities will be inadequate, if only because of the neighborhood effect involved in the fact that I benefit if another man contributes to the care of the insane. For this reason, we may be willing to arrange for their care through government.

Children offer a more difficult case. The ultimate operative unit in our society is the family, not the individual. Yet the acceptance of the family as the unit rests in considerable part on expediency rather than principle. We believe that parents are generally best able to protect their children and to provide for their development into responsible individuals for whom freedom is appropriate. But we do not believe in the freedom of parents to do what they will with other people. The children are responsible individuals in embryo, and a believer in freedom believes in protecting their ultimate rights.

To put this in a different and what may seem a more callous way, children are at one and the same time consumer goods and potentially responsible members of society. The freedom of individuals to use their economic resources as they want includes the freedom to use them to have children—to buy, as it were, the services of children as a particular form of consumption. But once this choice is exercised, the children have a value in and of themselves and have a freedom of their own that is not simply an extension of the freedom of the parents.

The paternalistic ground for governmental activity is in many ways the most troublesome to a liberal; for it involves the acceptance of a principle—that some shall decide for others—which he finds objectionable in most applications and which he rightly regards as a hallmark of his chief intellectual opponents, the proponents of collectivism in one or another of its guises, whether it be communism, socialism, or a welfare state. Yet there is no use pretending that problems are simpler than in fact they are. There is no avoiding the need for some measure of paternalism. As Dicey wrote in 1914 about an act for the protection of mental defectives, "The Mental Deficiency Act is the first step along a path on which no sane man can decline to enter, but which, if too far pursued, will bring statesmen across difficulties hard to meet without considerable interference with individual liberty."[1] There is no formula that can tell us where to stop. We must rely on our fallible judgment and, having reached a judgment, on our ability to persuade our fellow men that it is a correct judgment, or their ability to persuade us to modify our views. We must put our faith, here as elsewhere, in a consensus reached by imperfect and biased men through free discussion and trial and error.

Note

[1] A.V. Dicey, *Lectures on the Relation Between Law and Public Opinion in England During the Nineteenth Century* (2d ed.; London: Macmillan & Co., 1914), p. li.

Chapter Three

Medical Licensure

The overthrow of the medieval guild system was an indispensable early step in the rise of freedom in the Western world. It was a sign of the triumph of liberal ideas, and widely recognized as such, that by the mid-nineteenth century, in Britain, the United States, and to a lesser extent on the continent of Europe, men could pursue whatever trade or occupation they wished without the by-your-leave of any governmental or quasi-governmental authority. In more recent decades, there has been a retrogression, an increasing tendency for particular occupations to be restricted to individuals licensed to practice them by the state.

These restrictions on the freedom of individuals to use their resources as they wish are important in their own right. ...

I shall discuss ... restrictions on the practice of medicine. The reason for choosing medicine is that it seems desirable to discuss the restrictions for which the strongest case can be made—there is not much to be learned by knocking down straw men. I suspect that most people, possibly even most liberals, believe that it is desirable to restrict the practice of medicine to people who are licensed by the state. I agree that the case for licensure is stronger for medicine than for most other fields. Yet the conclusions I shall reach are that liberal principles do not justify licensure even in medicine and that in practice the results of state licensure in medicine have been undesirable. ...

The medical profession is one in which practice of the profession has for a long time been restricted to people with licenses. Offhand, the question, "Ought we to let incompetent physicians practice?" seems to admit of only a negative answer. But I want to urge that second thought may give pause.

In the first place, licensure is the key to the control that the medical profession can exercise over the number of physicians. To understand why this is so requires some discussion of the structure of the medical profession. The American Medical Association is perhaps the strongest trade union in the United States. The essence of the power of a trade union is its power to restrict the number who may engage in a particular occupation. This restriction may be exercised indirectly by being able to enforce a wage rate higher than would otherwise prevail. If such a wage rate can be enforced, it will reduce the number of people who can get jobs and thus indirectly the number of people pursuing the occupation. This technique of restriction has disadvantages. There is always a dissatisfied fringe of people who are trying to get into the occupation. A trade union is much better off if it can limit directly the number of people who enter the occupation—who ever try to get jobs in it. The disgruntled and dissatisfied are excluded at the outset, and the union does not have to worry about them.

The American Medical Association is in this position. It is a trade union that can limit the number of people who can enter. How can it do this? The essential control is at the stage of admission to medical school. The Council on Medical Education and Hospitals of the American Medical Association approves medical schools. In order for a medical school to get and stay on its list of approved schools it has to meet the standards of the Council. The power of the Council has been demonstrated at various times when there has been pressure to reduce numbers. For example, in the 1930s during the Depression, the Council on Medical Education and Hospitals wrote a letter to the various medical schools saying the medical schools were admitting more students than could be given the proper kind of training. In the next year or two, every school reduced the number it was admitting, giving very strong presumptive evidence that the recommendation had some effect.

Why does the Council's approval matter so much? If it abuses its power, why don't unapproved medical schools arise? The answer is that in almost every state in the United States, a person must be licensed to practice medicine, and to get the license, he must be a graduate of an approved school. In almost every state, the list of approved schools is identical with the list of schools approved by the Council on Medical Education and Hospitals of the American Medical Association. That is why the licensure provision is the key to the effective control of admission. It has a dual effect. On the one hand, the members of the licensure commission are always physicians and hence have some control at the step at which men apply for a license. This control is more limited in effectiveness than control at the medical school level. In almost all professions requiring licensure, people may try to get admitted more than once. If a person tries long enough and in enough jurisdictions he is likely to get through sooner or later. Since he has already spent the money and time to get his training, he has a strong incentive to keep trying. Licensure provisions that come into operation only after a man is trained therefore affect entry largely by raising the costs of getting into the occupation, since it may take a longer time to get in and since there is always some uncertainty whether he will succeed. But this rise in cost is nothing like so effective in limiting entry as is preventing a man from getting started on his career. If he is eliminated at the stage of entering medical school, he never comes up as a candidate for examination; he can never be troublesome at that stage. The efficient way to get control over the number in a profession is therefore to get control of entry into professional schools.

Control over admission to medical school and later licensure enables the profession to limit entry in two ways. The obvious one is simply by turning down many applicants. The less obvious, but probably far more important, one is by establishing standards for admission and licensure that make entry so difficult as to discourage young people from ever trying to get admission. Though most state laws require only two years of college prior to medical school, nearly one hundred percent of the entrants have had four years of college. Similarly, medical training proper has been lengthened, particularly through more stringent internship arrangements. ...

It is the provision about graduation from approved schools that is the most important source of professional control over entry. The profession has used this control to limit numbers. To avoid misunderstanding let me emphasize that I am not saying that individual members of the medical profession, the leaders of the medical profession, or the people who are in charge of the Council on Medical Education and Hospitals deliberately go out of their way to limit entry in order to raise their own incomes. That is not the way it works. Even when such people explicitly comment on the desirability of limiting numbers to raise incomes they will always justify the policy on the grounds that if "too" many people are let in, this will lower their incomes so that they will be driven to resort to unethical practices in order to earn a "proper" income. The only way, they argue, in which ethical practices can be maintained is by keeping people at a standard of income which is adequate to the merits and needs of the medical profession. I must confess that this has always seemed to me objectionable on both ethical and factual grounds. It is extraordinary that leaders of medicine should proclaim publicly that they and their colleagues must be paid to be ethical. And if it were so, I doubt that the price would have any limit. There seems little correlation between poverty and honesty. One would rather expect the opposite; dishonesty may not always pay but surely it sometimes does.

Control of entry is explicitly rationalized along these lines only at times like the Great Depression when there is much unemployment and relatively low incomes. In ordinary times, the rationalization for restriction is different. It is that the members of the medical profession want to raise what they regard as the standards of "quality" of the profession. The defect in this rationalization is a common one, and one that is destructive of a proper understanding of the operation of an economic system, namely, the failure to distinguish between technical efficiency and economic efficiency.

A story about lawyers will perhaps illustrate the point. At a meeting of lawyers at which problems of admission were being discussed, a colleague of mine, arguing against restrictive admission standards, used an analogy from the automobile industry. Would it not, he said, be absurd if the automobile industry were to argue that no one should drive a low quality car and therefore that no automobile manufacturer should be permitted to produce a car that did not come up to the Cadillac standard. One member of the audience rose and approved the analogy, saying that, of course, the country cannot afford anything but Cadillac lawyers! This tends to be the professional attitude. The members look solely at technical standards of performance, and argue in effect that we must have only first-rate physicians even if this means that some people get no medical service—though of course they never put it that way. Nonetheless, the view that people should get only the "optimum" medical service always leads to a restrictive policy, a policy that keeps down the number of physicians. I would not, of course, want to argue that this is the only force at work, but only that this kind of consideration leads many well-meaning physicians to go along with policies that they would reject out-of-hand if they did not have this kind of comforting rationalization.

It is easy to demonstrate that quality is only a rationalization and not the underlying reason for restriction. The power of the Council on Medical Education and Hospitals of the American Medical Association has been used to limit numbers in ways that cannot possibly have any connection whatsoever with quality. The simplest example is their recommendation to various states that citizenship be made a requirement for the practice of medicine. I find it inconceivable to see how this is relevant to medical performance. A similar requirement that they have tried to impose on occasion is that examination for licensure must be taken in English. A dramatic piece of evidence on the power and potency of the Association as well as on the lack of relation to quality is proved by one figure that I have always found striking. After 1933, when Hitler came to power in Germany, there was a tremendous outflow of professional people from Germany, Austria, and so on, including of course, physicians who wanted to practice in the United States. The number of physicians trained abroad who were admitted to practice in the United States in the five years after 1933 was the same as in the five years before. This was clearly not the result of the natural course of events. The threat of these additional physicians led to a stringent tightening of requirements for foreign physicians that imposed extreme costs upon them.

It is clear that licensure is the key to the medical profession's ability to restrict the number of physicians who practice medicine. It is also the key to its ability to restrict technological and organizational changes in the way medicine is conducted. The American Medical Association has been consistently against the practice of group medicine, and against prepaid medical plans. These methods of practice may have good features and bad features, but they are technological innovations that people ought to be free to try out if they wish. There is no basis for saying conclusively that the optimum technical method of organizing medical practice is practice by an independent physician. Maybe it is group practice, maybe it is by corporations. One ought to have a system under which all varieties can be tried.

The American Medical Association has resisted such attempts and has been able effectively to inhibit them. It has been able to do so because licensure has indirectly given it control of admission to practice in hospitals. The Council on Medical Education and Hospitals approves hospitals as well as medical schools. In order for a physician to get admission to practice in an "approved" hospital, he must generally be approved by his county medical association or by the hospital board. Why can't unapproved hospitals be set up? Because under present economic conditions, in order for a hospital to operate it must have a supply of interns. Under most state licensure laws, candidates must have some internship experience to be admitted to practice, and internship must be in an "approved" hospital. The list of "approved" hospitals is generally identical with that of the Council on Medical Education and Hospitals. Consequently, the licensure law gives the profession control over hospitals as well as over schools. This is the key to the AMA's largely successful opposition to various types of group practice. In a few cases, the groups have been able to survive. In the District of Columbia, they succeeded because they were able to bring suit against the American Medical Association under the federal Sherman antitrust laws, and won the suit. In a few other cases, they have succeeded for special reasons. There is, however, no doubt that the tendency toward group practice has been greatly retarded by the AMA's opposition.

It is interesting, and this is an aside, that the medical association is against only one type of group practice, namely, prepaid group practice. The economic reason seems to be that this eliminates the possibility of engaging in discriminatory pricing.[1]

It is clear that licensure has been at the core of the restriction of entry and that this involves a heavy social cost, both to the individuals who want to practice medicine but are prevented from doing so and to the public deprived of the medical care it wants to buy and is prevented from buying. Let me now ask the question: Does licensure have the good effects that it is said to have?

In the first place, does it really raise standards of competence? It is by no means clear that it does raise the standards of competence in the actual practice of the profession for several reasons. In the first place, whenever you establish a block to entry into any field, you establish an incentive to find ways of getting around it, and of course medicine is no exception. The rise of the professions of osteopathy and of chiropractic is not unrelated to the restriction of entry into medicine. On the contrary, each of these represented, to some extent, an attempt to find a way around restriction of entry. Each of these, in turn, is proceeding to get itself licensed, and to impose restrictions. The effect is to create different levels and kinds of practice, to distinguish between what is called medical practice and substitutes such as osteopathy, chiropractic, faith healing, and so on. These alternatives may well be of lower quality than medical practice would have been without the restrictions on entry into medicine.

More generally, if the number of physicians is less than it otherwise would be, and if they are all fully occupied, as they generally are, this means that there is a smaller total of medical practice by trained physicians—fewer medical man-hours of practice, as it were. The alternative is untrained practice by somebody; it may and in part must be by people who have no professional qualifications at all. Moreover, the situation is much more extreme. If "medical practice" is to be limited to licensed practitioners, it is necessary to define what medical practice is…. Under the interpretation of the statutes forbidding unauthorized practice of medicine, many things are restricted to licensed physicians that could perfectly well be done by technicians and other skilled people who do not have a Cadillac medical training. I am not enough of a technician to list the examples at all fully. I only know that those who have looked into the question say that the tendency is to include in "medical practice" a wider and wider range of activities that could perfectly well be performed by technicians. Trained physicians devote a considerable part of their time to things that might well be done by others. The result is to reduce drastically the amount of medical care. The relevant average quality of medical care, if one can at all conceive of the concept, cannot be obtained by simply averaging the quality of care that is given; that would be like judging the effectiveness of a medical treatment by considering only the survivors; one must also allow for the fact that the restrictions reduce the amount of care. The result may well be that the average level of competence in a meaningful sense has been reduced by the restrictions.

Even these comments do not go far enough, because they consider the situation at a point in time and do not allow for changes over time. Advances in any science or field often result from the work of one out of a large number of crackpots and quacks and people who have no standing in the profession. In the medical profession, under present circumstances, it is very difficult to engage in research or experimentation unless you are a member of the profession. If you are a member of the profession and want to stay in good standing in the profession, you are seriously limited in the kind of experimentation you can do. A "faith healer" may be just a quack who is imposing himself on credulous patients, but maybe one in a thousand or in many thousands will produce an important improvement in medicine. There are many different routes to knowledge and learning and the effect of restricting the practice of what is called medicine and confining it as we tend to do to a particular group, who in the main have to conform to the prevailing orthodoxy, is certain to reduce the amount of experimentation that goes on and hence to reduce the rate of growth of knowledge in the area. What is true for the content of medicine is true also for its organization, as has already been suggested. I shall expand further on this point below.

There is still another way in which licensure, and the associated monopoly in the practice of medicine, tend to render standards of practice low. I have already suggested that it renders the average quality of practice low by reducing the number of physicians, by reducing the aggregate number of hours available from trained physicians for more rather than less important tasks, and by reducing the incentive for research and development. It renders it low also by making it much more difficult for private individuals to collect from physicians for malpractice. One of the protections of the individual citizen against incompetence is protection against fraud and the ability to bring suit in the court against malpractice. Some suits are brought, and physicians complain a great deal about how much they have to pay for malpractice insurance. Yet suits for malpractice are fewer and less successful than they would be were it not for the watchful eye of the medical associations. It is not easy to get a physician to testify against a fellow physician when he faces the sanction of being denied the right to practice in an "approved" hospital. The testimony generally has to come from members of panels set up by medical associations themselves, always, of course, in the alleged interest of the patients.

When these effects are taken into account, I am myself persuaded that licensure has reduced both the quantity and quality of medical practice; that it has reduced the opportunities available to people who would like to be physicians, forcing them to pursue occupations they regard as less attractive; that it has forced the public to pay more for less satisfactory medical service, and that it has retarded technological development both in medicine itself and in the organization of medical practice. I conclude that licensure should be eliminated as a requirement for the practice of medicine.

When all this is said, many a reader, I suspect, like many a person with whom I have discussed these issues, will say, "But still, how else would I get any evidence on the quality of a physician. Granted all that you say about costs, is not licensure the only way of providing the public with some assurance of at least minimum quality?" The answer is partly that people do not now choose physicians by picking names at random from a list of licensed physicians; partly, that a man's ability to pass an examination twenty or thirty years earlier is hardly assurance of quality now; hence, licensure is not now the main or even a major source of assurance of at least minimum quality. But the major answer is very different. It is that the question itself reveals the tyranny of the status quo and the poverty of our imagination in fields in which we are laymen, and even in those in which we have some competence, by comparison with the fertility of the market. Let me illustrate by speculating on how medicine might have developed and what assurances of quality would have emerged, if the profession had not exerted monopoly power.

Suppose that anyone had been free to practice medicine without restriction except for legal and financial responsibility for any harm done to others through fraud and negligence. I conjecture that the whole development of medicine would have been different. The present market for medical care, hampered as it has been, gives some hints of what the difference would have been. Group practice in conjunction with hospitals would have grown enormously. Instead of individual practice plus large institutional hospitals conducted by governments or eleemosynary institutions, there might have developed medical partnerships or corporations—medical teams. These would have provided central diagnostic and treatment facilities, including hospital facilities. Some presumably would have been prepaid, combining in one package present hospital insurance, health insurance, and group medical practice. Others would have charged separate fees for separate services. And of course, most might have used both methods of payment.

These medical teams—department stores of medicine, if you will—would be intermediaries between the patients and the physician. Being long-lived and immobile, they would have a great interest in establishing a reputation for reliability and quality. For the same reason, consumers would get to know their reputation. They would have the specialized skill to judge the quality of physicians; indeed, they would be the agent of the consumer in doing so, as the department store is now for many a product. In addition, they could organize medical care efficiently, combining medical men of different degrees of skill and training, using technicians with limited training for tasks for which they were suited, and reserving highly skilled and competent specialists for the tasks they alone could perform. The reader can add further flourishes for himself, drawing in part, as I have done, on what now goes on at the leading medical clinics.

Of course, not all medical practice would be done through such teams. Individual private practice would continue, just as the small store with a limited clientele exists alongside the department store, the individual lawyer alongside the great many-partnered firm. Men would establish individual reputations and some patients would prefer the privacy and intimacy of the individual practitioner. Some areas would be too small to be served by medical teams. And so on.

I would not even want to maintain that the medical teams would dominate the field. My aim is only to show by example that there are many alternatives to the present organization of practice. The impossibility of any individual or small group conceiving of all the possibilities, let alone evaluating their merits, is the great argument against central governmental planning and against arrangements such as professional monopolies that limit the possibilities of experimentation. On the other side, the great argument for the market is its tolerance of diversity; its ability to utilize a wide range of special knowledge and capacity. It renders special groups impotent to prevent experimentation and permits the customers and not the producers to decide what will serve the customers best.

Note

[1] *See* Reuben Kessel, "Price Discrimination in Medicine," *The Journal of Law and Economics,* Vol. I (October 1958), pp. 20–53.

Chapter Four

Can the Consumer be Trusted?

> It is not from the benevolence of the butcher, the brewer, or the baker, that we expect our dinner, but from their regard to their own interest. We address ourselves, not to their humanity but to their self-love, and never talk to them of our own necessities but of their advantages. Nobody but a beggar chuses to depend chiefly upon the benevolence of his fellow citizens.
>
> —Adam Smith, *The Wealth of Nations,* vol. 1, p. 16

We cannot indeed depend on benevolence for our dinner—but can we depend wholly on Adam Smith's invisible hand? A long line of economists, philosophers, reformers, and social critics have said no. Self-love will lead sellers to deceive their customers. They will take advantage of their customers' innocence and ignorance to overcharge them and pass off on them shoddy products. They will cajole customers to buy goods they do not want. In addition, the critics have pointed out, if you leave it to the market, the outcome may affect people other than those directly involved. It may affect the air we breathe, the water we drink, the safety of the foods we eat. The market must, it is said, be supplemented by other arrangements in order to protect the consumer from himself and from avaricious sellers, and to protect all of us from the spillover neighborhood effects of market transactions.

These criticisms of the invisible hand are valid.... The question is whether the arrangements that have been recommended or adopted

Excerpts and notes from Chapter 7, "Who Protects the Consumer?" in *Free to Choose: A Personal Statement,* © 1990 by Milton Friedman and Rose D. Friedman, reprinted by permission of Harcourt Brace Jovanovich. All rights reserved.

to meet them, to supplement the market, are well devised for that purpose, or whether, as so often happens, the cure may not be worse than the disease.

This question is particularly relevant today. A movement launched less than two decades ago by a series of events—the publication of Rachel Carson's *Silent Spring,* Senator Estes Kefauver's investigation of the drug industry, and Ralph Nader's attack on the General Motors Corvair as "unsafe at any speed"—has led to a major change in both the extent and the character of government involvement in the marketplace—in the name of protecting the consumer. ...

Food and Drug Administration

...The Food and Drug Act of 1906 ... did not arise from protests over high prices, but from concern about the cleanliness of food. It was the era of the muckraker, of investigative journalism. Upton Sinclair had been sent by a socialist newspaper to Chicago to investigate conditions in the stockyards. The result was his famous novel, *The Jungle,* which he wrote to create sympathy for the workers, but which did far more to arouse indignation at the unsanitary conditions under which meat was processed. As Sinclair said at the time, "I aimed at the public's heart and by accident hit it in the stomach."

Long before *The Jungle* appeared and crystallized public sentiment in favor of legislation, such organizations as the Women's Christian Temperance Union and the National Temperance Society had formed the National Pure Food and Drug Congress (1898) to campaign for legislation to eliminate the medical nostrums of the day—mostly heavily laced with alcohol and so enabling spirits to be purchased and consumed in the guise of medicine, which explains the involvement of the temperance groups.

Here, too, special interests joined the reformers. The meat packers "learned very early in the history of the industry that it was not to their profit to poison their customers, especially in a competitive market in which the consumer could go elsewhere." They were especially concerned by restrictions on the importation of U.S. meat imposed by European countries, using as an excuse the allegation that the meat was diseased. They eagerly seized the opportunity to have the government certify that the meat was disease-free and at the same time pay for the inspection.[1]

Another special interest component was provided by the pharma-

cists and physicians through their professional associations, though
their involvement was more complex and less single-mindedly economic than that of the meat packers—or of the railroads in the establishment of the ICC.* Their economic interest was clear: patent medicines and nostrums, sold directly to the consumer by traveling
medicine men and in other ways, competed with their services. Beyond this, they had a professional interest in the kinds of drugs and
medicines available and were keenly aware of the dangers to the public
from useless medicines promising miraculous cures for everything
from cancer to leprosy. Public spirit and self-interest coincided.

The 1906 act was largely limited to the inspection of foods and
the labeling of patent medicines, though, more by accident than design, it also subjected prescription drugs to control, a power which was
not used until much later. The regulatory authority, from which the
present Food and Drug Administration developed, was placed in the
Department of Agriculture. Until the past fifteen years or so, neither
the initial agency nor the FDA had much effect on the drug industry.

Few important new drugs were developed until sulfanilamide
appeared in mid-1937. That was followed by the Elixir Sulfanilamide
disaster, which occurred as a result of a chemist's efforts to make sulfanilamide available to patients who were unable to take capsules. The
combination of the solvent he used and sulfanilamide proved deadly.
By the end of the tragedy "a hundred and eight people were dead—a
hundred and seven patients, who had taken the 'elixir,' and the chemist who had killed himself."[2] "Manufacturers themselves learned from
the ... experience the liability losses that could be suffered from the
marketing of such drugs and instituted premarketing safety tests to
avoid a repetition."[3] They also realized that government protection
might be valuable to them. The result was the Food, Drug, and Cos-
metic Act of 1938, which extended the government's control over
advertising and labeling and required all new drugs to be approved for
safety by the FDA before they could be sold in interstate commerce.
Approval had to be granted or withheld within 180 days.

A cozy symbiotic relation developed between the pharmaceutical
industry and the FDA until another tragedy occurred, the thalidomide
episode of 1961–62. Thalidomide had been kept off the U.S. market
by the FDA under the provisions of the 1938 act, though limited

---

*The Interstate Commerce Commission—the first regulatory agency created
by Congress (1887).

amounts of the drug have been distributed by physicians for experimental purposes. This limited distribution ended when reports surfaced about deformed babies born to European mothers who had taken thalidomide during pregnancy. The subsequent uproar swept into law in 1962 amendments that had developed out of Senator Kefauver's investigations of the drug industry the prior year. The tragedy also changed radically the thrust of the amendments. Kefauver had been concerned primarily with charges that drugs of dubious value were being sold at unduly high prices—the standard complaint about consumer exploitation by monopolistic business. As enacted, the amendments dealt more with quality than price. They "added a proof-of-efficacy requirement to the proof-of-safety requirement of the 1938 law, and they removed the time constraint on the FDA's disposition of a New Drug Application. No new drug may now be marketed unless and until the FDA determines that there is substantial evidence not only that the drug is safe, as required under the 1938 law, but that it is effective in its intended use."[4]

The 1962 amendments coincided with the series of events that produced an explosion in government intervention and a change in its direction: the thalidomide tragedy, Rachel Carson's *Silent Spring,* which launched the environmental movement, and the controversy about Ralph Nader's *Unsafe at Any Speed.* The FDA participated in the changed role of government and became far more activist than it had ever been before. The banning of cyclamates and the threat to ban saccharin have received most public attention, but they are by no means the most important actions of the FDA.

No one can disagree with the objectives of the legislation that culminated in the 1962 amendments. Of course it is desirable that the public be protected from unsafe and useless drugs. However, it is also desirable that new drug development should be stimulated, and that new drugs should be made available to those who can benefit from them as soon as possible. As is so often the case, one good objective conflicts with other good objectives. Safety and caution in one direction can mean death in another.

The crucial questions are whether FDA regulation has been effective in reconciling these objectives and whether there may not be better ways of doing so. These questions have been studied in great detail. By now, considerable evidence has accumulated that indicates that FDA regulation is counterproductive, that it has done more harm by retarding progress in the production and distribution of valuable drugs than it has done good by preventing the distribution of harmful or ineffective drugs.

The effect on the rate of innovation of new drugs is dramatic: the number of "new chemical entities" introduced each year has fallen by more than fifty percent since 1962. Equally important, it now takes much longer for a new drug to be approved and, partly as a result, the cost of developing a new drug has been multiplied manyfold. According to one estimate for the 1950s and early 1960s, it then cost about half a million dollars and took about twenty-five months to develop a new drug and bring it to market. Allowing for inflation since then would raise the cost to a little over one million dollars. By 1978, "it [was] costing $54 million and about eight years of effort to bring a drug to market"—a hundredfold increase in cost and quadrupling of time, compared with a doubling of prices in general.[5] As a result, drug companies can no longer afford to develop new drugs in the United States for patients with rare diseases. Increasingly, they must rely on drugs with high volume sales. The United States, long a leader in the development of new drugs, is rapidly taking a back seat. And we cannot even benefit fully from developments abroad because the FDA typically does not accept evidence from abroad as proof of effectiveness. The ultimate outcome may well be the same as in passenger rail traffic, the nationalization of the development of new drugs.

The so-called "drug lag" that has resulted is manifested in the relative availability of drugs in the United States and other countries. A careful study by Dr. William Wardell of the Center for the Study of Drug Development of the University of Rochester demonstrates, for example, that many more drugs are available in Great Britain that are not available in the United States than conversely, and that those available in both countries were on the average on the market sooner in Great Britain. Said Dr. Wardell in 1978,

> If you examine the therapeutic significance of drugs that haven't arrived in the United States but are available somewhere in the rest of the world, such as in Britain, you can come across numerous examples where the patient has suffered. For example, there are one or two drugs called Beta blockers, which it now appears can prevent death after a heart attack—we call this secondary prevention of coronary death after myocardial infarc-

tion—which, if available here, could be saving about 10,000 lives a year in the United States. In the ten years after the 1962 amendments, no drug was approved for hypertension—that's for the control of blood pressure—in the United States, whereas several were approved in Britain. In the entire cardiovascular area, only one drug was approved in the five-year period from 67 to 72. And this can be correlated with known organizational problems at FDA....

The implications for the patient are that therapeutic decisions that used to be the preserve of the doctor and the patient are increasingly being made at a national level, by committees of experts, and these committees and the agency for which they are acting—the FDA—are highly skewed towards avoiding risks so there's a tendency for us to have drugs that are safer but not to have drugs that are effective. Now I've heard some remarkable statements from some of these advisory committees where in considering drugs one has seen the statement "there are not enough patients with a disease of this severity to warrant marketing this drug for general use." Now that's fine if what you are trying to do is minimize drug toxicity for the whole population, but if you happen to be one of those "not enough patients," and you have a disease that is of high severity or a disease that's very rare, then that's just tough luck for you.

Granted all this, may these costs not be justified by the advantage of keeping dangerous drugs off the market, of preventing a series of thalidomide disasters? The most careful empirical study of this question that has been made, by Sam Peltzman, concludes that the evidence is unambiguous: that the harm done has greatly outweighed the good. He explains his conclusion partly by noting that "the penalties imposed by the marketplace on sellers of ineffective drugs before 1962 seems to have been sufficient to have left little room for improvement by a regulatory agency."[6] After all, the manufacturers of thalidomide ended up paying many tens of millions of dollars in damages—surely a strong incentive to avoid any similar episodes. Of course, mistakes will still happen—the thalidomide tragedy was one—but so will they under government regulation.

The evidence confirms what general reasoning strongly suggests. It is no accident that the FDA, despite the best of intentions, operates to discourage the development and prevent the marketing of new and potentially useful drugs.

Put yourself in the position of an FDA official charged with approving or disapproving a new drug. You can make two very different mistakes:

1. Approve a drug that turns out to have unanticipated side effects resulting in the death or serious impairment of a sizable number of persons.

2. Refuse approval of a drug that is capable of saving many lives or relieving great distress and that has no untoward side effects.

If you make the first mistake—approve a thalidomide—your name will be spread over the front page of every newspaper. You will be in deep disgrace. If you make the second mistake, who will know it? The pharmaceutical firm promoting the new drug, which will be dismissed as an example of greedy businessmen with hearts of stone, and a few disgruntled chemists and physicians involved in developing and testing the new product. The people whose lives might have been saved will not be around to protest. Their families will have no way of knowing that their loved ones lost their lives because of the "caution" of an unknown FDA official.

In view of the contrast between the abuse poured on the European drug companies that sold thalidomide and the fame and acclaim that came to the woman who held up approval of thalidomide in the United States (Dr. Frances O. Kelsey, given a gold medal for Distinguished Government Service by John F. Kennedy), is there any doubt which mistake you will be more anxious to avoid? With the best will in the world, you or I, if we were in that position, would be led to reject or postpone approval of many a good drug in order to avoid even a remote possibility of approving a drug that will have newsworthy side effects.

This inevitable bias is reinforced by the reaction of the pharmaceutical industry. The bias leads to unduly stringent standards. Getting approval becomes more expensive, time-consuming, and risky. Research on new drugs becomes less profitable. Each company has less to fear from the research efforts of its competitors. Existing firms and existing drugs are protected from competition. New entry is discouraged. Research that is done will be concentrated on the least controversial, which means least innovative, of the new possibilities.

When one of us suggested in a *Newsweek* column (January 8,

1973) that for these reasons the FDA should be abolished, the column evoked letters from persons in pharmaceutical work offering tales of woe to confirm the allegation that the FDA was frustrating drug development. But most also said something like, "In contrast to your opinion, I do not believe that the FDA should be abolished but I do believe that its power should be" changed in such and such a way.

A subsequent column, entitled "Barking Cats" (February 19, 1973), replied:

> What would you think of someone who said, "I would like to have a cat provided it barked"? Yet your statement that you favor an FDA provided it behaves as you believe desirable is precisely equivalent. The biological laws that specify the characteristics of cats are no more rigid than the political laws that specify the behavior of governmental agencies once they are established. The way the FDA now behaves, and the adverse consequences, are not an accident, not a result of some easily corrected human mistake, but a consequence of its constitution in precisely the same way that a meow is related to the constitution of a cat. As a natural scientist, you recognize that you cannot assign characteristics at will to chemical and biological entities, cannot demand that cats bark or water burn. Why do you suppose the situation is different in the social sciences?

The error of supposing that the behavior of social organisms can be shaped at will is widespread. It is the fundamental error of most so-called reformers. It explains why they so often feel that the fault lies in the man, not the "system"; that the way to solve problems is to "turn the rascals out" and put well-meaning people in charge. It explains why their reforms, when ostensibly achieved, so often go astray.

The harm done by the FDA does not result from defects in the people in charge—unless it be a defect to be human. Many have been able and devoted civil servants. However, social, political, and economic pressures determine the behavior of the people supposedly in charge of a government agency to a far greater extent than they determine its behavior. No doubt there are exceptions, but they are rare—almost as rare as barking cats.

That does not mean that effective reform is impossible. But it requires taking account of the political laws governing the behavior of government agencies, not simply berating officials for inefficiency and waste or questioning their motives and urging them to do better. The FDA did far less harm than it does now before the Kefauver amendments altered the pressures and incentives of the civil servants.

Notes

[1]Gabriel Kolko, *The Triumph of Conservatism* (The Free Press of Glencoe, 1963), quotation from p. 99.

[2]Richard Harris, *The Real Voice* (New York: Macmillan, 1964), p. 183.

[3]William M. Wardell and Louis Lasagna, *Regulation and Drug Development* (Washington, D.C.: American Enterprise Institute for Public Policy Research, 1975), p. 8.

[4]Sam Peltzman, *Regulation of Pharmaceutical Innovation* (Washington, D.C.: American Enterprise Institute for Public Policy Research, 1974), p. 9.

[5]Estimates for 1950s and early 1960s from Wardell and Lasagna, *Regulation and Drug Development*, p. 46; for 1978, from Louis Lasagna, "The Uncertain Future of Drug Development," *Drug Intelligence and Clinical Pharmacy*, vol. 13 (April 1979), p. 193.

[6]Peltzman, *Regulation of Pharmaceutical Innovation*, p. 45.

Chapter Five

Crime

"Lost is our old simplicity of times,
The world abounds with laws, and teems with crimes."
—On the Proceedings Against
America, Anonymous, 1775

The rising incidence of crime is surely one of the most troubling problems bedeviling American society in recent years. As government has undertaken more and more responsibilities, it had been performing one of its basic functions less and less well. If the first duty of a government is to defend the country against foreign enemies, the second duty is to prevent the coercion of one person by another and to provide security for its citizens and their property.

We are far richer today than in earlier days. We should be better able to secure person and property than we could when fewer resources were available to the nation. Yet the situation is the reverse. Crime has been rising. The average citizen feels less secure than at almost any time in the past hundred years.

We believe that the growth of government in recent decades and the rising incidence of crime in those same decades are largely two sides of the same coin. Crime has risen not *despite* government's growth but largely *because* of government's growth.

The number of violent crimes of all kinds has literally exploded in the past few decades. In 1957 ... violent crimes of all kinds numbered 199,000. From then to 1980 they multiplied more than sixfold, reaching 1,309,000. Allowing for the increase in population, the rate per 100,000 persons multiplied fivefold from 117 to 581. Over the same period, crimes against property increased even more rapidly, the rate per 100,000 persons multiplying more than sevenfold from 719 to 5,319.

Over the same period, public expenditures on law enforcement went from $2.7 billion to $25.9 billion, multiplying nearly tenfold. Since prices rose nearly threefold and population rose by one-third, expenditures on law enforcement per capita rose nearly threefold after allowing for inflation. Clearly, throwing money at the problem has been no more effective in curbing crime than in improving education…, or in achieving the fine objectives in the long list of social programs that have been undertaken over those decades. The number of arrests has also risen sharply—from two million in 1957 to nearly ten million in 1980. The rise in the number of arrests simply reflected the rise in the number of crimes committed, not a growing efficiency of law enforcement—the reported number of crimes grew even more rapidly than the number of arrests.

Why the Increase in Crime?

We are not criminologists. Criminologists themselves have no simple and easy explanations of the rapid increase in crime. Nonetheless, some popular explanations can be rejected out of hand, and some partial explanations are highly persuasive.

One popular explanation for crime is poverty and inequality. People are driven to steal, to rob, to murder because they have no other means to avoid hunger and deprivation. Or they are driven to crime because of the spectacle of rich versus poor, a spectacle that feeds a sense of injustice and unfairness, not to speak of the less admirable motive of envy. However plausible this explanation is of why some people turn to crime, it obviously cannot explain the *rise* in crime over recent decades in the United States. As a nation we are wealthier than we were fifty, seventy-five, or a hundred years ago, and that wealth is if anything more evenly distributed. Moreover, there is less poverty and less inequality in the United States than in many other countries. Poverty is certainly more prevalent, more degrading, more intolerable in India than in the United States, and unquestionably the spectacle of rich versus poor is more blatant. Yet, there is less chance of being mugged or robbed on the streets of Bombay or Calcutta at night than on the streets of New York or Chicago.

A closely related view is that the actual degree of poverty or the actual degree of inequality is less important than the *perceptions* of potential criminals, and that those perceptions have been greatly affected in the United States by some of the very technological developments that have been most responsible for the increasing well-being of the population at large, notably in communication and transportation—television, radio, and the like. Television programs, it is said, provide a picture of a lifestyle that the poor cannot hope to achieve by honest labor, yet is presented as something that everyone has a right to or that everyone can attain.

No doubt such perceptions do contribute to crime. After all, it would be inconsistent to regard the advertising that television carries for products as effective but ignore as ineffective the advertising that it carries for lifestyles and moral standards. Nonetheless, we find it hard to believe that a change in perceptions is more than a minor contributing cause of the enormous expansion in crime that has occurred in the past few decades.

Two factors seem to us more important, factors that we have associated … with the growth of government in general. One is the change in the climate of opinion, since the time of the New Deal, about the role of the individual and the role of government. That change shifted emphasis from individual responsibility to societal responsibility. It encouraged the view that people are the creatures of their environment and should not be held responsible for their behavior. In its extreme form, the view is that there is no such thing as "crime," that what is called criminal activity is a form of "illness" that calls for treatment rather than punishment.

If people who are poor hold the view that poverty is not their own fault but the fault of society at large, then it is perfectly understandable that their reaction is "Since society is responsible for my poverty, I have every right to act against society and to take what I need or want." Similarly, if they come to believe that the well-to-do whom they see on TV, or observe in high-income neighborhoods, are well-to-do not because of their own efforts—not because they worked hard or saved or in some way contributed to society—but simply because they happened to draw winning tickets in a social lottery, then it is easy to understand their believing that nothing is wrong in correcting the outcome of that lottery by taking property from others.

A closely associated development has been the change in the character of the family. Statistics on divorce, one-parent families, and illegitimate births demonstrate that the nuclear family is losing its traditional role. The family no longer serves as fully as it once did as an integrative institution, as a vehicle for instilling values and developing standards of behavior. Nothing has taken its place. As a result, an increasing number of our youth grow up without any firm values, with little understanding of "right" and "wrong," with few convictions that will discipline their appetites. This is all the more significant, as criminologists have long emphasized, because crime is disproportionately an activity of the young.

Another development that has unquestionably contributed to the rise in crime is the multiplication of laws and rules and regulations. *These have multiplied the number of actions that are crimes.* It is literally impossible for anyone to obey all the laws, since no one can possibly know what they are. Similarly, it is literally impossible for the legal authorities to enforce all the laws equally and without discrimination. To do so, the whole population would have to be employed to police itself. As a result, enforcement of the laws invariably becomes partly a matter of which laws the authorities choose to enforce and against whom—a situation hardly designed to encourage respect for the majesty of the law. We said in *Free to Choose:*

> When the law contradicts what most people regard as moral and proper, they will break the law—whether the law is enacted in the name of a noble ideal … or in the naked interest of one group at the expense of another. Only fear of punishment, not a sense of justice and morality, will lead people to obey the law.
>
> When people start to break one set of laws, the lack of respect for the law inevitable spreads to all laws, even those that everyone regards as moral and proper—laws against violence, theft, and vandalism (p. 145).

What to Do about It

Criminologists and others have made many suggestions for altering procedures for apprehending criminals, for indicting them, convicting them, sentencing them, incarcerating them, and so on. Many have urged controlling guns and other weapons to reduce their availability. We have no competence to discuss these proposed remedies. Instead, we can comment only on those aspects of the problem that are tied to our general theme of the importance of reducing government in order to promote the general welfare.

If we are right that the tide is turning, that public opinion is shifting away from a belief in big government and away from the doctrine of social responsibility, then that change will in the course of time tend to alter the circumstances to which we attribute much of the rise in crime. In particular, it will tend to restore a belief in individual responsibility by strengthening the family and reestablishing its traditional role in instilling values in the young.

Moreover, if there is a change in the tide, it will produce some institutional changes that will also contribute to a reduction in crime. In particular, the adoption of vouchers for schooling ... could have a major effect. It would offer the disadvantaged who now populate the urban slums greater educational opportunities for their children, giving them a wider and more desirable range of alternatives than street crime. However, any such institutional effects will take a long time to yield their fruits—decades, not years.

One set of changes that could yield relatively rapid results is a reduction in the acts that are regarded by the law as crimes. The most promising measure of this kind is with respect to drugs. Most crimes are not committed by people hungry for bread. By far more are committed by people hungry for dope. Should we have learned a lesson from Prohibition? When Prohibition was enacted in 1920, Billy Sunday, the noted evangelist and leading crusader against Demon Rum, greeted it as follows: "The reign of tears is over. The slums will soon be only a memory. We will turn our prisons into factories and our jails into storehouses and corncribs. Men will walk upright now, women will smile, and the children will laugh. Hell will be forever for rent." We know now how tragically wrong he was. New prisons and jails had to be built to house the criminals spawned by converting the drinking of spirits into a crime against the state. Prohibition undermined respect for the law, corrupted the minions of the law, and created a decadent moral climate—and in the end did not stop the consumption of alcohol.

Despite this tragic object lesson, we seem bent on repeating precisely the same mistake in handling drugs. There is no disagreement about some of the facts. Excessive drinking of alcohol harms the drinker; excessive smoking of cigarettes harms the smoker; excessive use of drugs harms the drug user. As among the three, awful as it is to make such comparisons, there is little doubt that smoking and drinking kill far more people than the use of drugs.

All three actions also have adverse effects on people *other than those who drink or smoke or use drugs.* Drunken driving accounts for a large number of all traffic accidents and traffic fatalities. Smoking harms nonsmoking occupants of the same aircraft, the same restaurant, the same public places. Drug users cause accidents when driving or when at work. According to a recent *Newsweek* article, "employees who use drugs on the job are one-third less productive than straight workers, three times as likely to be injured and absent far more often…. Starved, strung-out and coked-up employees affect the morale in the office, scare away customers and hurt the quality of the shirts you wear, the cars you drive and the building you work in."

Whenever we evaluate a government action, we must consider both whether the intended results of that action are ones that it is proper for government to seek to achieve and, further, whether the action will in fact achieve these results. The facts about alcohol, tobacco, and drugs raise two very different issues: one of ethics and one of expediency. The ethical question is whether we have the right to use the machinery of government to prevent individuals from drinking, smoking, or using drugs. Almost everyone would answer at least a qualified yes with respect to children. Almost everyone would answer an unqualified yes with respect to preventing users of alcohol or tobacco or drugs from inflicting harm on third parties. But with respect to the addicts themselves, the answer is far less clear. Surely, it is important and appropriate to reason with a potential addict, to tell him the consequences, to pray for, and with, him. But do we have the right to use force directly or indirectly to prevent a fellow adult from drinking, smoking, or using drugs? Our own answer is no. But we readily grant that the ethical issue is a difficult one and that men of goodwill often disagree.

Fortunately, we do not have to resolve the ethical issue to agree on policy because the answer to whether government action *can* prevent addiction is so clear. Prohibition—whether of drinking, smoking, or using drugs—is an attempted cure that in our judgment makes matters worse both for the addict and for the rest of us. Hence, even if you regard government measures to prohibit the taking of drugs as ethically justified, we believe that you will find that considerations of expediency make it unwise to adopt such measures.

Consider first the addict. Legalizing drugs might increase the number of addicts, though it is not certain that it would. Forbidden fruit is attractive, particularly to the young. More important, many persons are deliberately made into drug addicts by pushers, who now give likely prospects their first few doses free. It pays the pusher to do so because, once hooked, the addict is a captive customer. If drugs were legally available, any possible profit from such inhumane activity would largely disappear, since the addict could buy from a cheaper source.

Whatever happens to the total number of addicts—and the possible increase of that number—the *individual* addict would clearly be far better off if drugs were legal. Today, drugs are both extremely expensive and highly uncertain in quality. Addicts are driven to associate with criminals to get the drugs, and they become criminals themselves to finance the habit. They risk constant danger of death and disease.

Consider, next, the rest of us. The harm to us from the addiction of others arises primarily from the fact that drugs are illegal. It has been estimated that from one third to one half of all violent and property crime in the United States is committed either by drug addicts engaged in crime to finance their habit, or by conflicts among competing groups of drug pushers, or in the course of the importation and distribution of illegal drugs. Legalize drugs, and street crime would drop dramatically and immediately. Moreover, addicts and pushers are not the only ones corrupted. Immense sums are at stake. It is inevitable that some relatively low-paid police and other government officials—and some high-paid ones as well—succumb to the temptation to pick up easy money.

The clearest case is marijuana, the use of which has been becoming sufficiently widespread to mimic the pattern that developed under the prohibition of alcohol. In California, marijuana has become either the largest, or second largest, cash crop. In large areas of the state, law enforcement personnel wink at the growers and harvesters of marijuana in much the same way as law enforcement officials did at moonshiners and bootleggers in the 1920s. Special squads must be set up to fly the helicopters that locate marijuana fields and to make the raids that destroy them, just as in the 1920s, special squads were set up to enforce the prohibition of alcohol. And just as bootleggers had to protect themselves in the 1920s from hijackers, so now the marijuana growers must protect their illegal crop themselves. They post armed guards to protect the growing fields. Gun battles inevitably result, as they did under Prohibition.

Under Prohibition, both bootleggers and do-it-yourselfers producing bathtub gin sometimes used wood alcohol or other substances that made the product a powerful poison, leading to the injury and sometimes death of those who drank it. Currently, the same thing is happening in an even more reprehensible fashion. The U.S. government itself has persuaded some foreign governments to use airplanes to spray paraquat—a dangerous poison—on growing marijuana fields. It has itself done so recently in Georgia. The purpose is to make the marijuana unusable. But there is no way, apparently, to prevent some of the contaminated marijuana from coming on the market and harming those who use it. And there is no certainty that the aim of the helicopter pilots is sufficiently accurate to guarantee that no paraquat falls on plants other than marijuana.

There would be tremendous outcry if it were known that government officials had deliberately poisoned some of the food eaten by convicted criminals. Surely, it is a far more heinous and utterly unjustifiable practice to spread poison deliberately over crops likely to harm citizens who may or may not be innocent of breaking a law and who have never had their day in court.

Some proponents of the legalization of marijuana have argued that smoking marijuana does not cause harm. We are not competent to judge this much debated issue—though we find persuasive the evidence we have seen that marijuana is a harmful substance. Yet, paradoxical though it may seem, our belief that it is desirable to legalize marijuana and all other drugs does not depend on whether marijuana or other drugs are harmful or harmless. However much harm drugs do to those who use them, it is our considered opinion that seeking to prohibit their use does even more harm both to users of drugs and to the rest of us.

Legalizing drugs would simultaneously reduce the amount of crime and improve law enforcement. It is hard to conceive of any other single measure that would accomplish so much to promote law and order. But, you may say, must we accept defeat? Why not simply end the drug traffic? That is where experience both with Prohibition and, in recent years, with drugs is most relevant. We cannot end the drug traffic. We may be able to cut off opium from Turkey—but the opium poppy grows in innumerable other places. With French cooperation, we may be able to make Marseilles an unhealthy place to manufacture heroin—but the simple manufacturing operations can be carried out in innumerable other places. We may be able to persuade Mexico to spray or allow us to spray marijuana fields with paraquat— but marijuana can be grown almost everywhere. We may be able to cooperate with Colombia to reduce the entry of cocaine—but success is not easy to attain in a country where the export is a large factor in the economy. So long as large sums of money are involved—and they are bound to be if drugs are illegal—it is literally impossible to stop the traffic, or even to make a serious reduction in its scope.

In drugs, as in other areas, persuasion and example are likely to be far more effective than the use of force to shape others in our image.

Drug use is not the only area where crime could be reduced by legalizing activities that are now illegal, but it surely is the most obvious and the most important. Our emphasis here is based not only on the growing seriousness of drug-related crimes, but also on the belief that relieving our police and our courts from having to fight losing battles against drugs will enable their energies and facilities to be devoted more fully to combating other forms of crime. We could thus strike a double blow: reduce crime activity directly, and at the same time increase the efficacy of law enforcement and crime prevention.

Chapter Six

A War We're Losing

While we have just finished a war abroad, we are still engaged in one at home—the war on drugs. There was great concern—and properly so—about the casualties in the Gulf war. There seems to be far less concern about the casualties in the war on drugs, even though they are far more numerous than the casualties suffered during the Gulf war's entire course.

The war on drugs has many effects, some good, more, in my opinion, bad. I propose here to concentrate on a single effect, the cost in human lives.

The accompanying chart plots the homicide rate per 100,000 population from 1910 to 1989. (All figures are drawn from the *Statistical Abstract of the United States*, and *Historical Statistics of the United States*.) There was a steady rise through World War I, and then an even steeper rise when the Eighteenth Amendment prohibiting the production, distribution, and sale of alcoholic beverages became effective. That rise peaked in 1933, the year in which the Prohibition amendment was repealed. The homicide rate then fell, at first rapidly, and then more slowly to the mid-1950s, except for a brief but sharp rise during and after World War II—repeating the behavior during World War I. In the mid-1960s, the homicide rate started to rise, and then soared after the war on drugs was launched by President Nixon and continued by his successors.

The second series in the chart, the number of prisoners received, for which data are readily available to me only from 1925, confirms the effect of both alcoholic prohibition and drug prohibition on recorded criminality, though unlike the homicide rate, it has recently risen to far higher rates than during the 1930s.

The accompanying table shows the average rate of homicides and

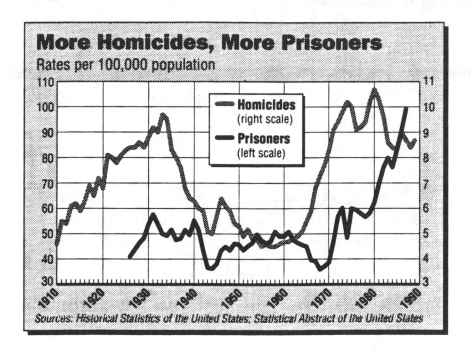

More Homicides, More Prisoners
Rates per 100,000 population

Homicides (right scale)

Prisoners (left scale)

Sources: Historical Statistics of the United States; Statistical Abstract of the United States

of prisoners received by decades from the 1950s on.

The difference between the homicide rate in the 1980s and in the 1950s, adjusted for the current population of the United States, implies almost 11,000 extra homicides per year; compared with the 1960s, more than 8,000. Similar estimates for prisoners received come to more than 80,000 extra prisoners compared with the 1950s, nearly 90,000 compared with the 1960s.

Granted that the whole of the difference may not be attributable to the war on drugs. Many other things were going on during the decades from the 50s to the 80s. However, there seems little doubt that the war on drugs is the single most important factor that produced such drastic increases. Even if only half the effect is attrib-

The Crime Boom
Average Rates per 100,000 population

DECADE	HOMICIDES	PRISONERS RECEIVED
1950-59	4.8	47.2
1960-69	5.7	43.7
1970-79	9.5	54.3
1980-89	9.1	79.7[1]

[1]1980-87

Sources: Historical Statistics of the United States; Statistical Abstract of the United States

uted to the war on drugs, 5,000 extra homicides a year and 45,000 extra prisoners is a high cost, and that price does not include the lives lost in Colombia, Peru, and elsewhere, because we cannot enforce our own laws, or the lives lost through adulterated drugs in a black market, or the culture of violence, disrespect for the law, corruption of law enforcement officials, and disregard of civil liberties unleashed by the war on drugs.

No doubt there have been some favorable effects of the war on drugs. There does appear to have been a considerable reduction in the casual use of drugs. But it is hard to believe that the good effects come anywhere close to being large enough to justify the human cost of the war on drugs in terms of lives lost and lives destroyed.

Chapter Seven

The Drug War as a Socialist Enterprise

In 1972, almost twenty years ago, President Nixon started a war on drugs—the first intensive effort to enforce the prohibition of drugs since the original Harrison Act. In preparation for this talk today, I re-read the column that I published in *Newsweek* criticizing his action.* Very few words in that column would have to be changed for it to be publishable today. The problem then was primarily heroin and the chief source of the heroin was Marseilles. Today, the problem is cocaine from Latin America. Aside from that, nothing would have to be changed.

Here it is almost twenty years later. What were then predictions are now observable results. As I predicted in that column, on the basis primarily of our experience with Prohibition, drug prohibition has not reduced the number of addicts appreciably if at all and has promoted crime and corruption.

Why is it that the only observable effect on policy of the conversion of predictions into results has been that the government digs itself deeper and deeper into a bigger and bigger hole and spends more and more of your and my money doing harm? Why is it? That's both the most discouraging feature of our experience and also the most intriguing intellectual puzzle.

In our private lives, if we try something and it goes awry, we don't just continue and do it on a bigger and bigger scale. We may for a while, but sooner or later we stop and change. Why does not the same thing happen in governmental policy?

This chapter is adapted from Prof. Friedman's keynote address presented at the Fifth International Conference on Drug Policy Reform in Washington, D.C., on Nov. 16, 1991.

*See Chapter 5, "Crime," pages 39–43 for a version of this column.

There is little point to my discussing in detail before this group the case for the legalization of drugs. Everyone in this room knows it. You have had numerous workshops featuring discussions by people who are more intimately familiar with the details than I am. I want rather to examine the puzzle that I raised. And in doing so, I'm going to rely on an adage that Bartlett traces back to 325 B.C.: "Cobbler, stick to your last."

My last is economics, the study of how society organizes its limited resources to meet the many and varied wants of its members. Fundamentally, society's resources can be organized in only one of two ways, or by some mixture of them.

One way is by market mechanisms: from the bottom up. The other way is by command: from the top down. The market is one mechanism. Authoritarian organization—the military is a clear example—is the other. The general gives the order, the colonel passes it on to the captain, and so on down the line. In the market, the orders come the other way. The consumer walks into a store and gives the order and the orders go up. These two mechanisms have very different characteristics and are suited to handle very different problems.

Some element of both mechanisms is needed in any society. And every society has some mixture of both. We know the extreme cases in which authoritarianism predominates and we know what happened in those extreme cases, particularly since the fall of the Berlin Wall. But we also have large elements of both mechanisms in our own society.

During the many years that I've been peripherally engaged in discussing the issue of drugs—I should emphasize that's not a vocation of mine; it's an avocation—I've been impressed by two things. First, most literature that I have read on drugs takes it for granted that the drug problem is a special case to be discussed in terms of specific issues associated with drugs—the substances involved and so on— rather than a special instance of a more general phenomenon. It is taken for granted that the drug problem has to be discussed in terms of its own merits and requires an extensive knowledge of the details.

From my point of view, it's as if one were to discuss the problem of theft in terms of the object stolen. So, theft of automobiles is one problem. Theft of hand bags is another. In the same way, people treat the prohibition of drugs as if it were a problem to itself.

Second, one consequence of that approach to the drug problem is that many opponents of the war on drugs propose alternatives that would be just as bad. They believe that the problem is not the basic mechanism being used, but simply that the government hasn't done it right. Most of these alternatives would involve going from the frying pan to the fire.

Such reformers believe that if they could write the law, the law would be enforced the way they wrote it. That is an illusion. What happens to a law has little relation, in general, to the intentions of the people who wrote it. The people who wrote the law on drugs did not intend to kill hundreds of thousands of people in the process. They did not intend to have a system under which prisons and prisoners would grow like Topsy. In general, the actual effects of any law are often, if not usually, the opposite of the intentions of the people who wrote it, a phenomenon that Congressman Richard Armey [R-Texas], in an earlier guise when he was a simple professor, termed the "invisible foot of government."

Let me illustrate with a few quotations from letters that I have received. First: "Instead of merely decriminalizing drugs, let's have the government make available drugs free to every user." That would obviously take the profit out of the business. The idea is that somehow or other we ought to treat drugs as a free good. But there are no free goods; there's no free lunch. It's not free; somebody would have to pay for it. So, we ought to tax the taxpayer to subsidize people who use drugs! More important, it seems obvious that if those "free" drugs were really available, they would be distributed in Europe and elsewhere where there's a paying market.

How can you restrict the quantity demanded of free drugs? The only way to do so is to have strict rules for distributing it. That leads to an authoritarian system determining who gets the drugs and how much—as open to abuse and corruption as our present system.

Second—I promise you, these are honest-to-God quotes from letters I have received; I haven't made them up—"Legalize all drugs now illegal to be available in state stores." We have a lot of experience with state stores in the liquor area. The Twenty-First Amendment repealing the Prohibition Amendment repealed only federal prohibition; states were left free to engage in any measures they wanted to control alcohol. Indeed, the Twenty-First Amendment specifies that transporting alcohol or liquor from a dry state to a wet state shall be regarded as a federal offense and shall be prevented by the federal government. Some states stayed dry, at least for a while; others set up state liquor stores; and still others left it to the market.

The people who say drugs should be distributed only in state stores argue that that would facilitate control of distribution to minors, to ensure that drugs weren't abused, and so on. Has that been the effect of state liquor stores? Hardly. I know about the state of New Hampshire best because we used to have a second home there. Some New Hampshire stores are located right on the border of Massachusetts in order to attract as many customers from Massachusetts as possible. As that indicates, state stores give government an incentive to promote, not discourage, the consumption of alcohol. In addition, many states have now discovered that they are not really doing very well with the state stores and there is a movement on to sell them off and privatize them. Again, it's a silly idea.

Third: "Abolish the criminality of the use of drugs; establish a federal monopoly to sell drugs." That is, you are going to have the Post Office handle the distribution of drugs.

What do these solutions have in common? They propose to cure a problem caused by socialism by some more socialism. It's the standard recourse of the alcoholic: more of the hair of the dog that bit you to get over the inevitable hangover.

The fundamental problem we face is not the war on drugs—although some of us are most interested in that issue. The war on drugs and the harm which it does are simply manifestations of a much broader problem: the substitution of political mechanisms for market mechanisms in a wide variety of areas.

To illustrate, I want to go beyond the war on drugs. We all recognize that the war on drugs is destroying our inner cities. But if I were to ask any one of you what is the next most important factor that is destroying the inner cities, I suspect a great many would agree with me that the next most important factor is our defective educational system, the terrible schools in our inner cities, schools which do not teach, but which are essentially places to keep kids off the streets for a certain number of hours a day.

Both failures have the same source. The war on drugs is a failure because it is a socialist enterprise. Our schooling is deteriorating because it is a socialist enterprise. Except possibly for the military, education is the largest socialist enterprise in the United States. There are a few loopholes: private schools to which parents can send their children if they can afford to pay or, in the case of parochial schools, if they have certain religious views. However, ninety percent of all kids are in government schools. And that socialist institution performs the same as most other socialist institutions.

There are some general features of a socialist enterprise, whether it's the Post Office, schools, or the war on drugs. The enterprise is inefficient, expensive, very advantageous to a small group of people, and harmful to a lot of people. That was true of socialism in Russia, it was true of socialism in Poland, and it's true of socialism in the United States.

You all know Adam Smith's famous invisible hand, in which people who intend to promote their own interest are led by an invisible hand to promote a public interest which it was no part of their intention to promote. I have for many years argued that an inversion of that maxim is also true: People who intend only to pursue the public interest are led by an invisible hand to promote private interests which it was no part of their intention to pursue. That is the case regarding drugs.

Whose interests are served by the drug war? The U.S. government enforces a drug cartel. The major beneficiaries from drug prohibition are the drug lords, who can maintain a cartel that they would be unable to maintain without current government policy.

In education, one major set of beneficiaries from the socialized educational system are high-income people, living in affluent suburbs, who are able to have good public schools. Those government schools serve as a tax shelter for them. If they send their children to private schools, the tuition they pay is not deductible in computing their federal income tax; but local taxes are deductible. Another set of beneficiaries are the educational bureaucracy, including officers and employees of teachers' unions, and politicians who are able to use the educational system as a source of patronage.

On the other hand, a great mass of people are harmed by the low and declining quality of our schooling system. And the people who are harmed worst of all are the people who live in the inner cities. They know it. In public opinion polls on privatizing the school system through vouchers that give parents freedom to choose, blacks are the most supportive group, with two-thirds or more favoring a voucher system. Yet, with the exception of Polly Williams of Wisconsin, not a single important black political leader has come out in favor of vouchers!

These are by no means the only examples. Go down the list of our major national concerns, of which the crime and lawlessness spawned by drug prohibition is certainly one and poor educational performance another. We have major problems in medical care. Total costs for medical care have risen from four percent of the national income to thirteen percent in forty years. Why? Again, because the government has increasingly socialized medical care and there is a very strong movement to go all the way to a complete socialization of medical care. Largely as a result of greater government involvement, the cost of a day spent in the hospital, cost per patient day, was twenty-six times as high in 1989, after adjustment for inflation, as it was in 1946.

Another example is housing. Why does the Bronx in New York look like a war zone that's just been bombed? Primarily because of rent control. Again, an attempt by the government to socialize the housing industry. We have had extensive and expensive public housing programs. In the course of those public housing programs, more dwelling units have been destroyed than have been built.

I challenge you to find any major problem in the United States that you cannot trace back to the misuse of political mechanisms as opposed to market mechanisms.

By any reasonable measure, the United States today is a little over fifty percent socialist. That is to say, more than fifty percent of the total resources in the country, of the total input, is directly or indirectly controlled by governmental institutions at all levels—federal, state, and local. Yet we in the United States have the highest standard of living of any country in the world. We are a very rich and prosperous country. It is an extraordinary tribute to the productivity of the market system that, with less than fifty percent of the resources, it can produce the kind of standard of living and the kind of society we have.

You are working from January 1 to close to June 30, or maybe somewhere after June 30, to pay for the direct and indirect cost of government. What fraction of your well-being comes from those government-controlled expenditures? Is it anything like fifty percent? I doubt very much that many of you would say it is.

The question that my puzzle raises is why is it that private enterprises are successful and government enterprises are not? One common answer is that the difference is in the incentive, that somehow the incentive of profit is stronger than the incentive of public service. In one sense, that's right; but in another, it's wrong.

The people who run our private enterprises and the people who run our government enterprises have exactly the same incentive. In both cases, they want to promote their private interests. The people who go into our government, who operate our government, are the same kind of people as those who are in the private sector. They are just as smart, in general. They have just as much integrity. They have just as many altruistic and selfless interests. There is no difference in that way. But as Armen Alchian, an economist at UCLA, once put it, "The one thing you can depend on everybody to do is to put his interest above yours." That is a very insightful comment.

The Chinese who are on the mainland are not different people from the Chinese who are in Hong Kong. Yet, the Mainland is a morass of poverty and Hong Kong has been an oasis of relative well-being. The people who occupied West Germany and East Germany before they were reunited had the same background, the same culture. They were the same people, but the results were drastically different.

The problem is not in the kind of people who run our governmental institutions versus those who run our private institutions. The trouble, as the Marxists used to say, is in the system. The system is what is at fault.

The difference is that the private interest of people is served in a different way in the private and the governmental spheres. Consider the bottom line they face.

Here's a project that might be suggested, to begin with, by somebody in the private sector or by somebody in the government sphere, and appears equally promising in either case. However, all good ideas are conjectures; they are experiments. Most are going to fail. What happens? Suppose a private group undertakes the project. Suppose it starts to lose money. The only way that they can keep it going is by digging into their own pockets. They have to bear the costs. That enterprise will not last long; people will shut it down. They will go on to something else.

Suppose government undertakes the same project and its initial experience is the same: it starts to lose money. What happens? The government officials could shut it down, but they have a very different alternative. With the best of intentions, they can believe that the only reason it has not done well is because it has not been operating on a large enough scale. They do not have to dig into their own pockets to finance an expansion. They can dig into the pockets of the taxpayers.

Indeed, financing an expansion will enable them to keep lucrative jobs. All they need to do is to persuade the taxpayers or the legislators who control the purse that their project is a good one. And they are generally able to do so because, in turn, the people who vote on the expansion are not voting their own money; they are spending somebody else's money. And nobody spends somebody else's money as carefully as he spends his own.

The end result is that when a private enterprise fails, it is closed down; when a government enterprise fails, it is expanded. Isn't that exactly what has been happening with drugs? With schooling? With medical care?

We are all aware of the deterioration in schooling. But are you aware that we are now spending per pupil, on the average, three times as much as we were thirty years ago, after adjustment for inflation? There's a general rule in government and bureaucratic enterprises: the more you put in, the less you get out.

As these socialized enterprises have broadened their reach, it has become more and more difficult for the public to control them. That's the fundamental problem we face in respect of drugs. How do we make the vested interests of the government change their policy?

As we have all discovered, that is not an easy job. The people running the drug program have a great deal more resources than we have. They can command the attention of the media to make reform or repeal seem not respectable, not reasonable. After all, they will say over and over, the people who urge the legalization of drugs are simply ignorant or naïve or don't understand what's going on. We, they will say, are the experts and know what works and what doesn't.

One way that has been effective in eliminating or reducing bad government programs is private competition. The Post Office used to be just as inefficient in delivering parcels as it is in delivering first-class mail. But because the postal statutes gave it a monopoly only on first-class mail, UPS was able to take away their business. Then Federal Express and similar enterprises took away much of their first-class business, and substitutes for mail such as fax emerged.

The same process is underway in drugs. Unfortunately, however, private competition is not an effective solution as long as the government completely prohibits some drugs—just as first-class postage proper is still a government monopoly, because it is illegal for private enterprises to offer similar general carrier services. In such areas, we do need to change the law.

My thesis can be expressed in two main points, and that is where I want to close and open up to questions from you. First, do not fool yourself into thinking that solutions will in fact work that simply involve changing the way the political mechanism is used. They will not escape the defects common to the political mechanism wherever it is used.

Let me emphasize, I am a limited-government libertarian, not an anarchist libertarian, though I have a great deal of sympathy for anarchist libertarians, including the fact that my son is one. However, the role I assign to the government is limited to defending the country, providing law and order, helping us to determine the rules under which we operate, and adjudicating disputes. This is a very limited range of responsibilities.

A major cost of the broader extension of governmental activity is that it prevents government from doing well those things that I believe only it can do effectively. When people talk about innocent victims of the war on drugs, they very often forget the people who suffer robberies, theft, murder—not because they are caught in the crossfires of drug battles, not because they are the victims of addicts who are trying to support their habit, but simply because so large a fraction of law enforcement resources are being used to try to control drugs that there are not enough resources left to prevent theft, burglary, and the rest in the community at large.

The second lesson I believe that we should learn, and it's probably the more important lesson, is that we are likely to make more progress against the war on drugs if we recognize that repealing drug prohibition is part of the broader problem of cutting down the scope and power of the government and restoring power to the people. If we treat drug prohibition as an isolated instance, maybe the effort to repeal it will be successful, as the effort to repeal alcohol prohibition was in the 1920s. But I believe that our chances of success are greater if we recognize that the failure of the war on drugs is part of a much broader problem, that the reason to end the war on drugs is also the reason to end the socialization of medicine, the socialization of schools, and so on down the list.

Questions and Answers

ARNOLD S. TREBACH: I have a two-part question, one from the floor and one with a bit of my own amendment. Should every produced good be subject to the free market? And the second part of the question was, if I look back at Adam Smith and once, with great foreboding, I read the book, I think Adam Smith accepted the idea of, as you say, a limited role for government, including the administration of justice and I think the phrase was "the common defense." Many drug warriors would claim that because of the unique nature of drugs, they fit properly within the administration of justice and the common defense.

PROFESSOR FRIEDMAN: On the first half of the question, I believe that there is a case for keeping certain things out of the market. I believe it's not desirable to have a market in atomic bombs. But the number and the list of things for which you can really justify prohibition is very limited. And the only justification is always in terms of the existence of innocent victims, not in terms of paternalistic concern.

The major effect of drug prohibition is to multiply the number of innocent victims, not to reduce them. That's why I don't think that any general rule you might have that some products, such as atomic bombs, hydrogen bombs, and a few things like that, should not be traded in the market applies to the case of drugs.

On the second question, I don't believe that if Adam Smith were here today he would agree with that interpretation you gave to his strictures. The reason why the prohibition of drugs is not a case of the administration of justice is because the drug user, whether he's smart or foolish or not, harms primarily himself. There is a case for doing something when the drug user harms other people, and we do. The case of alcohol is very simple. The person who drives when he's drunk clearly should be prosecuted for that. It's the act of driving while drunk, not the act of drinking, for which he should be prosecuted. Similarly, if people under the influence of drugs do a similar thing, the act of doing that is what should be prosecuted, not the ingestion of drugs.

I've always argued that there are two arguments against drug prohibition. One is from principle: that people ought to be responsible for themselves and the government has no business telling me what to ingest. I'm sure this is the argument you've heard very effectively from Dr. Szasz.

The other is the question of expediency. For a moment, waive the question of principle. Are you doing more harm than good? The evidence that you are seems to me so overwhelming that it appeals to people who will not join you on matters of principle. I give you some examples.

My fundamental attitude toward drug prohibition initially developed out of the issue of principle. My good friend Bill Buckley was initially in favor of drug prohibition. In fact, my son David once wrote an article attacking Bill's views on prohibition under the title "Is Bill Buckley a Communicable Disease?" Bill had argued in favor of drug prohibition on the ground that one drug user would transmit his addiction to others, and in that way infect them. David said in his piece that Bill's ideas infect others. To take that to an extreme case—I don't think this was David's example; it's mine—Karl Marx's *Das Kapital* surely has ended up killing more people than have ever been killed by alcohol, tobacco, and so-called illegal drugs combined. But our principles of free speech say people ought to be free to read Marx. And that was what David meant by his "Is Bill Buckley a Communicable Disease?"

Well, Bill has switched and he is now a very strong proponent of drug legalization, not on grounds of principle but on grounds of expediency, on the ground that the effort has failed and ought to be terminated.

I don't believe there's any way in which you can say that the prohibition of drugs is administering justice. Justice to whom? Is it justice to the people of Colombia who are being murdered because we can't enforce our own laws? That's hardly justice.

TREBACH: I wasn't saying that. I was wondering if Adam Smith would. I know how you feel about...

FRIEDMAN: [*Simultaneously*] I know. No, I don't think Adam Smith would. Adam Smith was a very great man, a very smart man.

TREBACH: This question says you supported Pinochet or advised Pinochet.

FRIEDMAN: I never advised Pinochet. I never supported Pinochet.

TREBACH: We'll throw that one away.

FRIEDMAN: But hold on. No, I don't want to evade the question.

TREBACH: All right.

FRIEDMAN: Chile was a case in which a military regime, headed by Pinochet, was willing to switch the organization of the economy from a top-down to a bottom-up mode. In that process, a group of people who had been trained at the University of Chicago in the Department of Economics, who came to be called the Chicago Boys, played a major role in designing and implementing the economic reforms.

The real miracle in Chile was not that those economic reforms worked so well, because that's what Adam Smith said they would do. Chile is by all odds the best economic success story in Latin America today. The real miracle is that a military junta was willing to let them do it.

As I said to begin with, the principle of the military is from the top down. The principle of a market is from the bottom up. It's a real miracle that a military group was willing to let a bottom-up approach take over. I did make a trip to Chile and I gave talks in Chile. In fact, I did meet with Mr. Pinochet, but I never was an adviser to him, and I never got a penny from the Chilean government. But I will say that that process led to a situation in which you were able to get an election which ended the military junta. You now have a democratic government in Chile. There is as yet no similar example from the world of entirely socialist states.

So, I was not an adviser to Pinochet. I was not an adviser to the Chilean government, but I am more than willing to share in the credit for the extraordinary job that our students did down there.

TREBACH: I believe you were a supporter of Ronald Reagan.

FRIEDMAN: I still am, but not of everything that he did.

TREBACH: OK. The real question is—as I say, I was grouping these together—How do you feel about his drug war? I think I know the answer, or we know the answer.

FRIEDMAN: The answer is clear. I think that the drug war was a mistake. There are two areas in which I think the Reagan administration performed very badly. One was the drug war and the other was foreign trade. In the case of foreign trade, he laid the groundwork, unfortunately, for what has become a protectionist drive and movement by agreeing to the so-called voluntary import quotas on Japanese cars. That was an enormous mistake, went against all of his stated principles.

As I once said to a Republican Club of students at Stanford, I am a libertarian with a small *l* and a Republican with a capital *R*. And I am a Republican with a capital *R* on grounds of expediency, not on principle. I believe that I can do more good by having influence with the

Republican Party than I can by joining the Libertarian Party, although I have great sympathy with the Libertarian Party. I believe it's very desirable that they do well.

Ronald Reagan was a man of principle. He is the first president in my life who was elected because the people had come around to agreeing with him, rather than because he was looking at polls and saying what the people wanted to hear. He was saying exactly the same thing in 1980 when he was nominated, as he was in 1964 when he supported Mr. Goldwater. What changed was not what he was saying, but what the public had come to believe. His fundamental principle—that government is too big, that government is a problem—is correct. Unfortunately, the war on drugs was inconsistent with that fundamental principle and he should not have departed from it by supporting the war on drugs.

I may say to you also that I would have no hesitancy to say that to Ronald Reagan. You know, people have a great misconception about Mr. Reagan. They think that somehow he only listens to what he wants to hear, but that's not true.

TREBACH: There are several questions along this line. In light of the objective standing of the U.S. below the EEC by every standard— that is, the European countries—that measures quality of life and the reality that every EEC country is socialist, how can you argue for laissez-faire capitalism or, this says, robber baron—robber bandit, free market capitalism as a path, you know, for a better life for all Americans?

FRIEDMAN: I understand it. Well, I'm delighted that you have some socialists in this organization.

TREBACH: We have a few.

FRIEDMAN: When I talk to you about drug legalization, I'm talking to the converted. But when I'm talking to you about socialism, I'm not talking to the converted, so I'm being more useful.

In the first place, I do not agree with the factual statement in that remark. I do not agree that the EEC countries have a better quality of life in general. The typical difference between the EEC countries and the United States is that the United States is a country of much greater diversity and most of the EEC countries have relatively homogeneous populations. In almost all cases, the few immigrants they have are a great cause of trouble. You won't find a Turk in Germany or a Moroccan in France who will subscribe to the view that life is better in the EEC countries than it is in the United States, while we in the United States have a much greater variety and have been much more open and welcome to people.

In the second place, when you come to measure socialism, there's little more than a dime's worth of difference between the degree of socialism in those countries and in this. The major difference is that those countries, some of them, have more government-owned and operated enterprises. That's the major difference. Our only government-owned and operated enterprise is the Post Office. On the other hand, our government has extended its influence in considerable measure primarily by regulation and rules and restrictive arrangements. And in that case, far more so than most of the European countries.

In an issue that's very closely related to the drug issue, our Food and Drug Administration is a much more restrictive and socialist enterprise than its counterparts in England and other countries, as is evidenced by the drug lag. In general, it takes a good deal longer to get a drug approved for use in the United States than it does in Britain or Canada or Germany. Indeed, that's another case in which what's intended to save people's lives is killing far more people than it is saving, namely, our Food and Drug Administration, which I am in favor of abolishing.

So, I don't agree that those countries are very much more socialist. What I do think is a very different thing, and I'll go back to Adam Smith for this.

TREBACH: Good idea.

FRIEDMAN: When Cornwallis was defeated at Yorktown in the Revolutionary War, a young man came to Adam Smith and said that it was going to be the ruination of Britain. Adam Smith replied, "Young man, there's a deal of ruin in a nation." Now what do I mean by that? I mean that we have the highest standard of living, in reality, of any country in the world.

AUDIENCE MEMBER: For the few.

FRIEDMAN: Not for the few, for the many. I beg your pardon. We have a more equal distribution of income, in general, than most of the countries you're talking about. The distribution of income... [*Audience members making inaudible statements*] I'm sorry, I couldn't hear most of it.

TREBACH: Excuse me. Would you mind sending your questions up? The mike isn't picking it up, so please cool it.

FRIEDMAN: Somebody shouted out, "For the few, not for the many." It is true that there are a few who have enormously high incomes. Too many of them. But the fact is that when I speak about the level of living, I am speaking about the level of living of the great majority of the people in the country.

There's inequality of income in every country. Those inequalities are far greater in socialist countries than they are in capitalist countries. If you compare the level of living of people at the top and people at the bottom, the difference was much wider, for example, in the pre-collapsed Soviet Union than it is in the United States.

The issue of distribution of income is a very serious and important issue and it's worth discussing; I don't mean it isn't. But I think that the statement I have made is correct for the great bulk of the American people. The evidence is simple. How do people best vote? With their feet. Where do people try to immigrate? Some people do try to get into the European countries. In particular, the people from the former communist countries try to get into the less socialist countries of Western Europe. But so far as the United States is concerned, people from all over the world seek to immigrate here. They aren't coming here to be made miserable. They aren't coming here to be exploited. And you can't say that they're all fools; they know what they're getting into.

So, I reject the idea that this is a country in which a few stand on the backs of the multitudes, which is a standard argument of the Marxists.

Well, I'm glad to see there are a few non-socialists here, too.

TREBACH: It's very clear, simply from the applause, that the Drug Policy Foundation attracts a very wide range of opinions on all manners of things.

FRIEDMAN: And so you should.

TREBACH: Thank you. This may well be the last question, sir. There have been several like this. Looking at the future, in a market of retail sales, of re-legalized drugs, what do you think of the suggestions that have been made about how you model those reforms? For example, one of our board of directors members, Lester Grinspoon of Harvard, has suggested a harmfulness tax based upon the relative harmfulness of the drugs. Senator Galiber of the New York State Senate, who is here, put in a bill that would have made all the illegal drugs—all of them—available legally, but would have regulated them like alcohol. They've used precisely the alcohol model. For example, you could get the drug if you were an adult; you couldn't have the retail store near a school, etc. What thoughts do you have on the future?

FRIEDMAN: There is no chance whatsoever in the near future or the distant future of getting what I would really like, which is a free market. As a first step on the right road, I believe the right thing to do is to treat drugs, currently illegal drugs, exactly the same way you treat alcohol and tobacco. Not because that's the best way, not because that's the ideal arrangement, but because it's an arrangement that people know, that is in existence. It involves, in a certain sense, the least kind of change, so that the law you've described by Senator Galiber seems to me the right direction in which to go—right direction in the sense again of a practical compromise, not of ultimate principle.

Chapter Eight

On Liberty and Drugs

T *his chapter is adapted from an interview on "America's Drug Forum," a national public affairs talk show that appears on public television stations. Randy Paige is an Emmy Award-winning drug reporter from Baltimore, Maryland.*

PAIGE: Let us deal first with the issue of legalization of drugs. How do you see America changing for the better under that system?

FRIEDMAN: I see America with half the number of prisons, half the number of prisoners, ten thousand fewer homicides a year, inner cities in which there's a chance for these poor people to live without being afraid for their lives, citizens who might be respectable who are now addicts not being subject to becoming criminals in order to get their drug, being able to get drugs for which they're sure of the quality. You know, the same thing happened under prohibition of alcohol as is happening now.

Under prohibition of alcohol, deaths from alcohol poisoning, from poisoning by things that were mixed in with the bootleg alcohol, went up sharply. Similarly, under drug prohibition, deaths from overdose, from adulterations, from adulterated substances have gone up.

PAIGE: How would legalization adversely affect America, in your view?

FRIEDMAN: The one adverse effect that legalization might have is that there very likely would be more people taking drugs. That's not by any means clear. But, if you legalized, you destroy the black market, the price of drugs would go down drastically. And as an economist, lower prices tend to generate more demand. However, there are some very strong qualifications to be made to that.

The effect of criminalization, of making drugs criminal, is to drive people from mild drugs to strong drugs.

The show upon which this chapter is based is entitled "Milton Friedman: On Liberty and Drugs," no. 223 (1991).

PAIGE: In what way?

FRIEDMAN: Marijuana is a very heavy, bulky substance and, therefore, it's relatively easy to interdict. The warriors on drugs have been more successful interdicting marijuana than, let's say, cocaine. So, marijuana prices have gone up, they've become harder to get. There's been an incentive to grow more potent marijuana and people have been driven from marijuana to heroin, or cocaine, or crack.

PAIGE: Let us consider another drug then, and that is the drug crack.

FRIEDMAN: Crack would never have existed, in my opinion, if you had not had drug prohibition. Why was crack created? The preferred method of taking cocaine, which I understand was by sniffing it, snorting it, became very expensive and they were desperate to find a way of packaging cocaine...

PAIGE: The entrepreneurs.

FRIEDMAN: Of course, they're entrepreneurs. The people who are running the drug traffic are no different from the rest of us, except that they have more entrepreneurial ability and less concern about not hurting other people. They're more irresponsible in that way. But they're in a business and they're trying to make as much as they can. And they discovered a good way to make money was to dilute this crack with baking soda or whatever else—I mean, cocaine, whatever else they do—I don't know the procedure—so that they could bring it out in five dollar and ten dollar doses.

PAIGE: Let's talk about that more in a minute. But with regard to crack, considering the fact that it's very addictive and considering the fact that...

FRIEDMAN: That's very dubious. It is addictive, but I understand from all the medical evidence that it's no more addictive than other drugs. In fact, the most addictive drug everybody acknowledges is tobacco.

PAIGE: Well, let me rephrase that then. All of the information I've seen on it suggests that it is a drug which is very pleasurable.

FRIEDMAN: Absolutely, no doubt.

PAIGE: And the effect of it is also very short.

FRIEDMAN: Yes.

PAIGE: And it is very expensive because multiple doses cost a lot of money. My question is: If drugs were legalized and if crack cocaine were available at a low cost, could it not be devastating in that it is so pleasurable, I am told, that more people could get it and stay on it for longer periods of time?

FRIEDMAN: Well, maybe. Nobody can say with certainty what will happen along those lines. But I think it's very dubious, because all of the experience with legal drugs is that there's a tendency for people to go from the stronger to the weaker and not the other way around, just as you go from regular beer to light beer. That's the tendency that there is: from cigarettes without filters to low-tar, filtered cigarettes, and so on. But I can't rule out that what you're saying might happen, but, and this is a very important but, the harm that would result from that would be much less than it is now, for several reasons. The really main thing that bothers me about the crack is not what you're talking about, it's the crack babies, because that's the real tragedy. They are innocent victims. They didn't choose to be crack babies any more than the people who are born with the fetal alcohol syndrome.

PAIGE: As you know, we are already experiencing epidemic proportions of that. One out of four babies going into one hospital, I can tell you, in Maryland is addicted.

FRIEDMAN: But I'll tell you, it isn't that crack babies are necessarily addicted, but they tend to come in at low birth weight, they tend to come in mentally impaired, and so on. But you know that the number who do that from alcohol is much greater. So, the same problem arises there. That's what bothers me.

Now suppose you legalized. Under current circumstances, a mother who is a crack addict and is carrying a baby is afraid to go get prenatal treatment because she turned herself into a criminal, she's subject to being thrown into jail. Under legalized drugs, that inhibition would be off. And, you know, even crack addicts, mothers, have a feeling of responsibility to their children.

And I have no doubt that under those circumstances, it would be possible to have a much more effective system of prenatal care, a much more effective system of trying to persuade people who are on drugs not to have children or to go off drugs while they have children.

PAIGE: Let us turn to the early genesis of your belief that the drug laws may not be working the way the nation would hope them to. Tell me about the elements that you saw early on that changed your mind or changed your way of thinking.

FRIEDMAN: Well, I'm not saying *changed*. I would rather say *formed* my way of thinking, because I do not recall at any time that I was ever in favor of prohibition of either alcohol or drugs. I grew up—I'm old enough to have lived through some part of the Prohibition era.

PAIGE: And you remember it.

FRIEDMAN: I remember the occasion when a fellow graduate student at Columbia from Sweden wanted to take me downtown to a restaurant for a Swedish meal and introduced me to the Swedish drink aquavit. This was a restaurant at which this Swedish fellow had been getting aquavit all during Prohibition; they had been selling it to him. And this was just after the repeal of Prohibition. We went there and he asked them for some aquavit. They said, "Oh, no, we haven't gotten our license yet." And finally, he talked to them in Swedish and persuaded them to take us into the back where they gave us a glass of aquavit apiece. Now that shows the absurdity of it.

Prohibition was repealed in 1933 when I was twenty-one years old, so I was a teenager during most of Prohibition. Alcohol was readily available. Bootlegging was common. Any idea that alcohol prohibition was keeping people from drinking was absurd. There were speakeasies all over the place. But more than that. We had this spectacle of Al Capone, of the hijackings, of the gang wars. ...

Anybody with two eyes to see could see that this was a bad deal, that you were doing more harm than good. In addition, I became an economist. And as an economist, I came to recognize the importance of markets and of free choice and of consumer sovereignty and came to discover the harm that was done when you interfered with them. The laws against drugs were passed in 1914, but there was no very great enforcement of it.

PAIGE: That was the Harrison Act?

FRIEDMAN: The Harrison Act. There was no very great enforcement of it until after World War II, by which time I had been able to see the harmful effects of price control, of rent control, of other attempts for government to interfere with market things. So, it never occurred to me to be in favor of it.

PAIGE: Was there any single event, anything you happened to witness that made an impression upon you or was it ...

FRIEDMAN: No, there was no single event. It was a cumulative effect.

PAIGE: Of course, you know that there are those who say that when Prohibition was over with, consumption dramatically increased and that it would be a…

FRIEDMAN: I beg your pardon, that's simply not true. That's not a fact. What is true…

PAIGE: It has been argued. That has been argued.

FRIEDMAN: You have statistically reported figures in the books on the amount of alcohol consumed. That went up sharply right after Prohibition, but that was *illegal* alcohol consumption. If you take, as I have done, the chart of alcohol consumption before and after Prohibition, alcohol consumption after Prohibition came back roughly to where it was before and, over the course of the period since then, if anything, alcohol consumption has been going down not in absolute terms, but relative to the population and relative to the growth of income.

For a time, it went up rather slowly, along with income, with one exception. During World War II, it shot way up. But that's what happened during World War I. Of course, you never would have gotten Prohibition if you hadn't had all the young men away in France when the vote was taken, so that the women had an extraordinary influence on it. But the same thing happened during World War II. And then after World War II, it settled down again. And more recently, the consumption of alcohol has been going down on a per capita basis. So, it simply is not true that there was a tremendous increase.

So far as drugs itself is concerned, some years ago, Alaska legalized marijuana. Consumption of marijuana among high school students in Alaska went down. The Dutch, in Holland, do not prosecute soft drugs, like marijuana, and they would prefer not to prosecute hard drugs, but they feel impelled by the international obligations they've entered into, and consumption of marijuana by young people has gone down. And, equally more interesting, the average age of the users of hard drugs has gone up, which means they're not getting any more new recruits.

So, the evidence is very mixed. But I have to admit that the one negative feature of legalizing drugs is that there might be some additional drug addicts. However, I want to qualify that in still another way.

The child who's shot in a slum in a pass-by shooting, in a random shooting, is an innocent victim in every respect of the term. The person who decides to take drugs for himself is not an innocent victim. He has chosen himself to be a victim. And I must say I have very much less sympathy for him. I do not think it is moral to impose heavy costs on other people to protect people from their own choices.

PAIGE: For us to understand the real root of those beliefs, how about if we just talk for a minute about free market economic perspective, and how you see the proper role of government in its dealings with the individual.

FRIEDMAN: The proper role of government is exactly what John Stuart Mill said in the middle of the nineteenth century in *On Liberty*. The proper role of government is to prevent other people from harming an individual. Government, he said, never has any right to interfere with an individual for that individual's own good.

The case for prohibiting drugs is exactly as strong and as weak as the case for prohibiting people from overeating. We all know that overeating causes more deaths than drugs do. If it's in principle OK for the government to say you must not consume drugs because they'll do you harm, why isn't it all right to say you must not eat too much because you'll do harm? Why isn't it all right to say you must not try to go in for skydiving because you're likely to die? Why isn't it all right to say, "Oh, skiing, that's no good, that's a very dangerous sport, you'll hurt yourself"? Where do you draw the line?

PAIGE: Well, I would bet that former drug czar William Bennett, some other folks along those lines, would probably suggest that the present sale and distribution of illegal drugs is, in fact, an enterprise which harms another person and the government has to step in...

FRIEDMAN: [*Simultaneously*] It does harm a great many...

PAIGE: ...to protect the vulnerable.

FRIEDMAN: It does harm a great many other people, but primarily because it's prohibited. There are an enormous number of innocent victims now. You've got the people whose purses are stolen, who are bashed over the head by people trying to get enough money for their next fix. You've got the people killed in the random drug wars. You've got the corruption of the legal establishment. You've got the innocent victims who are taxpayers who have to pay for more and more prisons, and more and more prisoners, and more and more police. You've got the rest of us who don't get decent law enforcement because all the law enforcement officials are busy trying to do the impossible.

And, last, but not least, you've got the people of Colombia and Peru and so on. What business do we have destroying and leading to the killing of thousands of people in Colombia because we cannot enforce our own laws? If we could enforce our laws against drugs, there would be no market for these drugs. You wouldn't have Colombia in the state it's in.

PAIGE: Is it not true that the entire discussion here, the entire drug problem is an economic problem to…

FRIEDMAN: No, it's not an economic problem at all, it's a moral problem.

PAIGE: In what way?

FRIEDMAN: I'm an economist, but the economics problem is strictly tertiary. It's a moral problem. It's a problem of the harm which government is doing.

I have estimated statistically that the prohibition of drugs produces, on the average, ten thousand additional homicides a year. It's a moral problem that the government is going around killing ten thousand people. It's a moral problem that the government is making into criminals people, who may be doing something you and I don't approve of, but who are doing something that hurts nobody else. Most of the arrests for drugs are for possession by casual users.

Now here's somebody who wants to smoke a marijuana cigarette. If he's caught, he goes to jail. Now is that moral? Is that proper? I think it's absolutely disgraceful that our government, supposed to be our government, should be in the position of converting people who are not harming others into criminals, of destroying their lives, putting them in jail. That's the issue to me. The economic issue comes in only for explaining why it has those effects. But the economic reasons are not the reasons.

Of course, we're wasting money on it. Ten, twenty, thirty billion dollars a year, but that's trivial. We're wasting that much money in many other ways, such as buying up crops that ought never to be produced.

PAIGE: There are many who would look at the economics—how the economics of the drug business is affecting America's major inner cities, for example.

FRIEDMAN: Of course, it is, and it is because it's prohibited. See, if you look at the drug war from a purely economic point of view, the role of the government is to protect the drug cartel. That's literally true.

PAIGE: Is it doing a good job of it?

FRIEDMAN: Excellent. What do I mean by that?

In an ordinary free market business—let's take potatoes, beef, anything you want—there are thousands of importers and exporters. Anybody can go into the business. But it's very hard for a small person to go into the drug importing business because our interdiction efforts essentially make it enormously costly. So, the only people who can survive in that business are these large Medellín cartel kind of people who have enough money so they can have fleets of airplanes, so they can have sophisticated methods, and so on.

In addition to which, by keeping goods out and by arresting, let's say, local marijuana growers, the government keeps the price of these products high. What more could a monopolist want? He's got a government who makes it very hard for all his competitors and who keeps the price of his products high. It's absolutely heaven.

PAIGE: Of course, you know that there are conspiracy theorists who suggest it's there for a reason, and that's because governments are in cahoots with the drug runners; you wouldn't say that.

FRIEDMAN: No, it's not. I don't say that at all. You know, over and over again in government policy, good intentions go awry. And the reason good intentions go awry is because you're spending somebody else's money. And...

PAIGE: Have you ever shared these thoughts with former President Ronald Reagan?

FRIEDMAN: No, I've never shared these thoughts. He knows what my position is on drugs. But I never have had a specific discussion with them on these. I wish I had.

PAIGE: [*Simultaneously*] How about—Really? What would you have told him or what would you have liked to have told him about this issue?

FRIEDMAN: Exactly what I've said to you on this program. I would have liked to tell him that the intentions are fine, but the actual effect of the program was going to do far more harm than good. I would simply have given him the *Newsweek* column that I wrote in 1972 and asked him if he would read it. That's what I really would have done.

PAIGE: And President Bush?

FRIEDMAN: The same thing. President Bush, in a certain way, would have been less sympathetic I believe than Ronald Reagan would have been.

PAIGE: Why is that?

FRIEDMAN: Because Ronald Reagan is a man of principles, who

among his principles is a free market, among his principles is the idea that people ought to be responsible for themselves. President Bush is of a different character. He's got a background of a life spent in government. He has no major principles of the same kind about domestic policy, as he's shown by his behavior. Mr. Bush, in his two years, three years in office, has reversed every one of Ronald Reagan's proposals.

People talk about the Reagan-Bush administration. That's a bunch of nonsense. You had a Reagan administration and you've got a Bush administration. And in the economic area, Mr. Bush has reversed every one of the major planks of Mr. Reagan. Mr. Reagan's major plank was cutting tax rates; Mr. Bush has raised them. Deregulating? Bush has re-regulated them. Restraining government spending? Government spending has been going up like mad under Mr. Bush. So, you've got a program of reverse Reaganomics and it's going to bring us trouble, just as Reaganomics brought us a good period.

PAIGE: Let's deal with that briefly, because there are some who would say that, as one of the architects for the Reagan administration's economic policies, we now see the country in a very difficult...

FRIEDMAN: It's not because of...

PAIGE: ...adjusting. Did you make a big mistake?

FRIEDMAN: No, siree. The 1980s, the period from 83 to 88 and on was the longest peacetime expansion. It produced a great many new jobs. You forget that at the end of that period, the inflation rate was less than half of what it was at the beginning. The interest rate was less than half of what it was at the beginning. Unemployment was less than half of what it was at the beginning. That was a very good period.

The reason we're in trouble now, in my opinion, is primarily because Mr. Bush has reversed Reagan's policies. He made a promise to the taxpayers which he did not live up to.

PAIGE: So, where do you see it going now?

FRIEDMAN: I am very pessimistic about the immediate future of the American economy.

PAIGE: Many would say that a lot of your theories are grounded in the notion of personal interest; if it is in an individual's personal interest to do something, he or she will do that.

FRIEDMAN: That's not a theory, and there's nobody who will deny it. Is there anybody who will deny that you can expect every person to pursue his own personal interests? Now those personal interests don't have to be narrow. Mother Theresa is pursuing her own personal interest just as much as Donald Trump is pursuing his. But they're both pursuing their personal interest.

PAIGE: Some would say that that notion—that personal interest is what propels societies as well as people—is a heartless philosophy and that the underclass would not fare well under that kind of a notion. You've heard that before.

FRIEDMAN: Yes, of course. But the evidence is so overwhelming. The only countries in the world in which low income people have managed to get a halfway decent level of living are those which rely on capitalist markets. Just compare the quality of life, the level of living of the ordinary people in Russia and the ordinary people in, I won't say the United States, but in France, in Italy, in Germany, in England, or in Hong Kong. Compare Hong Kong with mainland China.

Every society is driven by personal interest. Mainland China is driven by personal interest. The question is: How is personal interest disciplined? If the only way you can satisfy your personal interest is by getting something that other people want to pay for. You've got to…

PAIGE: Or by forcing it down other people's throats at the point of a gun, I suppose.

FRIEDMAN: If you can do it.

PAIGE: At the extreme.

FRIEDMAN: At the extreme. But that won't get their cooperation. You may be able to kill them. You may be able to take their wealth. But it won't create any more wealth. So, the only societies which have been able to create broadly based relative prosperity have been those societies which have relied primarily on capitalist markets. That's true whether you take Hong Kong versus mainland China, East Germany versus West Germany, Czechoslovakia before World War II and currently. You cannot find a single exception to that proposition.

Adam Smith put it best over two hundred years ago, when he said people who intend only to pursue their self-interest are led by an invisible hand to promote the public interest even though that was no part of their intention. Mr. Ford did not develop the Ford car for the public interest. He did it for his private interest.

PAIGE: But Adam Smith also saw a role for government, for example, in the administration of justice, didn't he?

FRIEDMAN: So do I. I am not a zero government person. I think there is a real role of government. And one of the reasons I object to so many of the things that government has gotten into is that it prevents government from performing its proper role. A basic role of government is to keep you from having your house burgled, to keep you from being hit over the head. And because the larger fraction of our law enforcement machinery is devoted to the war on drugs, you haven't got that kind of safety.

PAIGE: But, of course, there is clearly the argument that if the police come and pick up a person who is addicted to a drug and does not have the money to buy those drugs, then they're also taking a potential burglar off the street who's going to come and get my house, right?

FRIEDMAN: They are, but they'll be more of them coming on, as we know, and besides what are you going to do with them. Are you going to house them? A majority of those people who are arrested are simply arrested for possession, they're casual users.

PAIGE: However, the sixty-five, seventy-five-year-old woman who looks out her window and sees drug dealers out in the street and she sees them carrying guns and selling drugs thirty feet from her front door has a right to call the police and say, "I want these people off the street."

FRIEDMAN: Absolutely.

PAIGE: And police should take them off the street. Correct?

FRIEDMAN: Absolutely. But it's a mistake to have a law which makes that the main function of the police. I don't blame the police. I don't blame that woman. I don't blame the drug dealers.

PAIGE: In what way?

FRIEDMAN: We put them in a position where that's the thing to do. When we say to a young man in the ghetto, "Look, if you get a reasonable job at McDonald's or anyplace else, you'll make five, six, seven dollars an hour. But on the other hand, here's this opportunity to peddle drugs in the street." Why does the juvenile have the opportunity? Because the law is easier on juveniles than it is on adults.

PAIGE: But how would you see legalization affecting the poor in this country?

FRIEDMAN: The poor? It depends on which poor. But in the main, legalization as such would not have a major effect on the poor. It would provide better opportunities for the poor by rendering the inner cities safe and a place where you might have some decent, proper businesses. It would provide an opportunity to do more to improve schooling. The deterioration of the schooling, which is another case of ineffective socialism, has as much to do with the problems in the inner city as drugs do. Drugs aren't the only thing at work.

But I don't believe legalization should be viewed primarily as a way to help the poor. Legalization is a way to stop—in our forum as citizens—a government from using our power to engage in the immoral behavior of killing people, taking lives away from people in the United States, in Colombia and elsewhere, which we have no business doing.

PAIGE: So, you see the role of the government right now as being just as deadly as if Uncle Sam were to take a gun to somebody's head.

FRIEDMAN: That's what he's doing, of course. Right now Uncle Sam is not only taking a gun to somebody's head, he's taking his property without due process of law. The drug enforcers are expropriating property, in many cases of innocent people on whom they don't have a real warrant. We're making citizens into spies and informers. We tell people call up, you don't have to give your name, just give your suspicions. That's a terrible way to run what's supposed to be a free country.

PAIGE: Let us turn in the final few minutes then to specifically what your vision is then. Under your system, if you could make a wish and have it come true, what system would that be? How would you legalize drugs? How would you go about doing that?

FRIEDMAN: I would legalize drugs by subjecting them to exactly the same rules that alcohol and cigarettes are subjected to now. Alcohol and cigarettes cause more deaths than drugs do, by far, from use, but many fewer innocent victims. And the major innocent victims, in that case, are the people who are killed by drunk drivers. And we ought to enforce the law against drunk driving, just as we ought to enforce the law against driving under the influence of marijuana, or cocaine, or anything else.

But I would, as a first step at least, treat the drugs exactly the way we now treat alcohol and tobacco, no different.

PAIGE: You know what Representative Charles Rangel [D-New York] would say.

FRIEDMAN: I have heard Charles Rangel. He's a demagogue, who has had no relationship between what he says and the interests of his own constituents. His own constituents, the people he serves, are among the people who would be benefited the most by legalization of drugs. Charles Rangel is pursuing his own self-interest.

PAIGE: Forgive me for throwing out a name, but I just wanted to mention a typical response to that would be if you treat it like alcohol, you're talking about full-page ads in magazines with cocaine. You're talking about television advertisers. You're talking about buying cocaine…

FRIEDMAN: I beg your pardon. Television advertising is forbidden today for alcohol.

PAIGE: For hard liquor, that's all.

FRIEDMAN: For hard liquor. And I say treat this the same way as you would treat alcohol. So, presumably such ads would be forbidden for this.

But, of course, in any event I'm not prohibiting anybody from reading Mr. Rangel, and his ideas are at least as dangerous as those full-page ads you're talking about.

PAIGE: What scares you the most about the notion of drugs being legal?

FRIEDMAN: Nothing scares me about the notion of drugs being legal.

PAIGE: Nothing.

FRIEDMAN: What scares me is the notion of continuing on the path we're on now, which will destroy our free society, making it an uncivilized place. There's only one way you can really enforce the drug laws currently. The only way to do is to adopt the policies of Saudi Arabia, Singapore, which some other countries adopt, in which a drug addict is subject to capital punishment or, at the very least, having his hand chopped off. If we were willing to have penalties like that—but would that be a society you'd want to live in?

PAIGE: Do these notions seem obvious to you?

FRIEDMAN: Yes. I have thought about them for a long time. I have observed behavior in this country and in other countries for a long time. And I find it almost incredible how people can support the present system of drug prohibition. It does so much more harm than good.

PAIGE: If it is obvious, why is it that you're in such a minority, particularly among…?

FRIEDMAN: Of course. Very good question. And the answer is because there are so many vested interests that have been built up behind the present drug war. Who are the people who are listened to about drugs? The people who have the obligation to enforce drug laws. They think they're doing the right thing. They're good human beings. Everybody thinks what he's doing is worth doing. Nobody is doing it for evil motives. But it's the same thing all over the government. Tell me, why is it so hard to get people to understand that it's stupid. To make sugar in the United States costs twice as much as in other countries.

PAIGE: Wouldn't you agree that fear is one of the strongest supports for the existing drug laws? Fear that, without them, the bottom would fall out.

FRIEDMAN: Yes, but it's a fake fear and it's a fear that is promoted. Listen to what the former drug czar, Mr. Bennett, said. First of all, he stated that consumption of alcohol after Prohibition has gone up three or fourfold or something. He was wrong, just factually wrong. He's made all sorts of scare talk about how many new addicts there would be. He's never provided a single bit of evidence, never provided any examples of any other place or anything. But why? Because he's got a job to do.

PAIGE: Vested interests, you're saying.

FRIEDMAN: Vested interests, self-interest, the same self-interest that people object to in the market. But in the market, if you start a project and it goes wrong, you have to finance it out of your own pocket.

PAIGE: Last question. You have grandchildren.

FRIEDMAN: Absolutely.

PAIGE: You have a two-year-old granddaughter.

FRIEDMAN: Yes.

PAIGE: And her name is?

FRIEDMAN: Her name is Becca.

PAIGE: When you look at Becca, what do you see for her and for her future?

FRIEDMAN: That depends entirely on what you and your fellow citizens do to our country. If you and your fellow citizens continue on moving more and more in the direction of socialism, not only inspired through your drug prohibition, but through the socialization of schools, the socialization in medicine, the regulation of industry, I see for my granddaughter the equivalent of Soviet communism three years ago.

PAIGE: Do you worry about drugs affecting your granddaughter somehow?

FRIEDMAN: I don't worry about drugs, but I worry about government doing something about drugs. I do not worry about her getting addicted to drugs. She has good parents. Her parents will provide her with good role models...

PAIGE: I just mean the violence surrounding the drug trade, just the...

FRIEDMAN: The violence is due to prohibition and nothing else. How much violence is there surrounding the alcohol trade? There's some, only because we prohibit the sale of alcohol to children, which we should do, and there's some because we impose very high taxes on alcohol and, as a result, there's some incentive for bootlegging. But there's no other violence around it.

Part Two

Thomas
Szasz

Chapter Nine

The Control of Conduct: Authority vs. Autonomy

There is only one political sin: independence; and only one political virtue: obedience. To put it differently, there is only one offense against authority: self-control; and only one obeisance to it: submission to control by authority.

Why is self-control, autonomy, such a threat to authority? Because the person who controls himself, who is his own master, has no need for an authority to be his master. This, then, renders authority unemployed. What is he to do if he cannot control others? To be sure, he could mind his own business. But this is a fatuous answer, for those who are satisfied to mind their own business do not aspire to become authorities. In short, authority needs subjects, persons not in command of themselves—just as parents need children and physicians need patients.

Autonomy is the death knell of authority, and authority knows it: hence the ceaseless warfare of authority against the exercise, both real and symbolic, of autonomy—that is, against suicide, against masturbation, against self-medication, against the proper use of language itself![1]

The parable of the Fall illustrates this fight to the death between control and self-control. Did Eve, tempted by the Serpent, seduce Adam, who then lost control of himself and succumbed to evil? Or did Adam, facing a choice between obedience to the authority of God and his own destiny, choose self-control?

How, then, shall we view the situation of the so-called drug abuser or drug addict? As a stupid, sick, and helpless child, who, tempted by pushers, peers, and the pleasures of drugs, succumbs to

Chapter 12 from *Ceremonial Chemistry: The Ritual Persecution of Drugs, Addicts, and Pushers* is reprinted with permission of Learning Publications, Inc. Copyright 1989 by Thomas S. Szasz. All rights reserved.

the lure and loses control of himself? Or as a person in control of himself, who, like Adam, chooses the forbidden fruit as the elemental and elementary way of pitting himself against authority?

There is no empirical or scientific way of choosing between these two answers, of deciding which is right and which is wrong. The questions frame two different moral perspectives, and the answers define two different moral strategies: If we side with authority and wish to repress the individual, we shall treat him *as if* he were helpless, the innocent victim of overwhelming temptation; and we shall then "protect" him from further temptation by treating him as a child, slave, or madman. If we side with the individual and wish to refute the legitimacy and reject the power of authority to infantilize him, we shall treat him *as if* he were in command of himself, the executor of responsible decisions; and we shall then demand that he respect others as he respects himself by treating him as an adult, a free individual, or a "rational" person.

Either of these positions makes sense. What makes less sense— what is confusing in principle and chaotic in practice—is to treat people as adults *and* children, as free and unfree, as sane and insane.

Nevertheless, this is just what social authorities throughout history have done: in ancient Greece, in medieval Europe, in the contemporary world, we find various mixtures in the attitudes of the authorities toward the people; in some societies, the individual is treated as more free than unfree, and we call these societies "free"; in others, he is treated as more determined than self-determining, and we call these societies "totalitarian." In none is the individual treated as completely free. Perhaps this would be impossible: many persons insist that no society could survive on such a premise consistently carried through. Perhaps this is something that lies in the future of mankind. In any case, we should take satisfaction in the evident impossibility of the opposite situation: no society has ever treated the individual, nor perhaps could it treat him, as completely determined. The apparent freedom of the authority, controlling both himself and subject, provides an irresistible model: if God can control, if pope and prince can control, if politician and psychiatrist can control—then perhaps the person can also control, at least himself.

The conflicts between those who have power and those who want to take it away from them fall into three distinct categories. In moral, political, and social affairs (and I of course include psychiatric affairs among these), these categories must be clearly distinguished; if we do not distinguish among them we are likely to mistake opposition to absolute or arbitrary power with what may, actually, be an attempt to gain such power for oneself or for the groups or leaders one admires.

First, there are those who want to take power away from the oppressor and give it to the oppressed, as a class—as exemplified by Marx, Lenin, and the Communists. Revealingly, they dream of the "dictatorship" of the proletariat or some other group.

Second, there are those who want to take power away from the oppressor and give it to themselves as the protectors of the oppressed—as exemplified by Robespierre in politics; Rush in medicine; and by their liberal, radical, and medical followers. Revealingly, they dream of the incorruptibly honest or incontrovertibly sane ruler leading his happy or healthy flock.

And third, there are those who want to take power away from the oppressor and give it to the oppressed as individuals, for each to do with as he pleases, but hopefully for his own self-control—as exemplified by Mill, von Mises, the free market economists, and their libertarian followers. Revealingly, they dream of people so self-governing that their need for and tolerance of rulers is minimal or nil.

While countless men say they love liberty, clearly only those who, by virtue of their actions, fall into the third category, mean it.[2] The others merely want to replace a hated oppressor by a loved one—having usually themselves in mind for the job.

Psychiatrists (and some other physicians, notably public health administrators) have traditionally opted for "reforms" of the second type; that is, their opposition to existing powers, ecclesiastic or secular, has had as its conscious and avowed aim the paternalistic care of the citizen-patient and not the freedom of the autonomous individual. Hence, medical methods of social control tended not only to replace religious methods, but sometimes to exceed them in stringency and severity. In short, the usual response of medical authority to the controls exercised by non-medical authority has been to try to take over and then escalate the controls, rather than to endorse the principle and promote the practice of removing the controls by which the oppressed are victimized.

As a result, until recently, most psychiatrists, psychologists, and other behavioral scientists had nothing but praise for the "behavioral controls" of medicine and psychiatry. We are now beginning to witness, however, a seeming backlash against this position, many behavioral scientists jumping on what they evidently consider to be the next "correct" and "liberal" position, namely, a criticism of behavioral controls. But since most of these "scientists" remain as hostile to individual freedom and responsibility, to choice and dignity, as they have always been, their criticism conforms to the pattern I have described above: they demand more "controls"—that is, professional and governmental controls—over "behavior controls." This is like first urging a person to drive over icy roads at breakneck speed to get over them as fast as possible, and then, when his car goes into a skid, advising him to apply his brakes. Whether because they are stupid or wicked or both, such persons invariably recommend fewer controls where more are needed, for example in relation to punishing offenders—and more controls where fewer are needed, for example in relation to contracts between consenting adults. Truly, the supporters of the Therapeutic State are countless and tireless—now proposing more therapeutic controls in the name of "controlling behavior controls."[3]

Clearly, the seeds of this fundamental human propensity—to react to the loss of control, or to the threat of such loss, with an intensification of control, thus generating a spiraling symbiosis of escalating controls and counter-controls—have fallen on fertile soil in contemporary medicine and psychiatry and have yielded a luxuriant harvest of "therapeutic" coercions. The alcoholic and Alcoholics Anonymous, the glutton and Weight Watchers, the drug abuser and the drug-abuseologist—each is an image at war with its mirror image, each creating and defining, dignifying and defaming the other, and each trying to negate his own reflection, which he can accomplish only by negating himself.

There is only one way to split apart and unlock such pairings, to resolve such dilemmas—namely, by trying to control the other less, not more; and by replacing control of the other with self-control.

The person who uses drugs—legal or illegal drugs, with or without a physician's prescription—may be submitting to authority, may be revolting against it, or may be exercising his own power of making a free decision. It is quite impossible to know—without knowing a great deal about such a person, his family and friends, and his whole cultural setting—just what such an individual is doing and why. But it is quite possible, indeed it is easy, to know what those persons who try to repress certain kinds of drug uses and drug users are doing and why.

As the war against heresy was in reality a war for "true" faith, so the war against drug abuse is in reality a war for "faithful" drug use: concealed behind the war against marijuana and heroin is the war for tobacco and alcohol; and, more generally, concealed behind the war against the use of politically and medically disapproved drugs, is the war for the use of politically and medically approved drugs.

Let us recall ... one of the principles implicit in the psychiatric perspective on man, and some of the practices that follow from it: the madman is a person lacking adequate internal controls over his behavior; hence, he requires—for his own protection as well as for the protection of society—external restraints upon it. This, then, justifies the incarceration of "mental patients" in "mental hospitals"—and much else besides.

The drug abuser is a person lacking adequate internal controls over his drug use; hence, he requires—for his own protection as well as for the protection of society—external restraints upon it. This, then, justifies the prohibition of "dangerous drugs," the incarceration and involuntary treatment of "addicts," the eradication of "pushers"—and much else besides.

Confronted with the phenomena of "drug abuse" and "drug addiction," how else could psychiatry and a society imbued with it have reacted? They could respond only as they did—namely, by defining the moderate use of legal drugs as the result of the sane control of resistible impulses; and by defining the immoderate use of any drug, and any use of illegal drugs, as the insane surrender to irresistible impulses. Hence the circular psychiatric definitions of drug habits, such as the claim that illicit drug use (for example, smoking marijuana) causes mental illness and also constitutes a symptom of it; and the seemingly contradictory claim that the wholly similar use of licit drugs (for example, smoking tobacco) is neither a cause nor a symptom of mental illness.

Formerly, opium was a panacea; now it is the cause and symptom of countless maladies, medical and social, the world over. Formerly masturbation was the cause and symptom of mental illness; now it is the cure for social inhibition and the practice ground for training in heterosexual athleticism. It is clear, then, that if we want to understand and accept drug-taking behavior, we must take a larger view of the so-called drug problem. (Of course, if we want to persecute "pushers" and "treat addicts," then information inconvenient to our doing these things will only get in our way. Drug-abuseologists can no more be "educated" out of their coercive tactics than can drug addicts.)

What does this larger view show us? How can it help us? It shows us that our present attitudes toward the whole subject of drug use, drug abuse, and drug control are nothing but the reflections, in the mirror of "social reality," of our own expectations toward drugs and toward those who use them; and that our ideas about and interventions in drug-taking behavior have only the most tenuous connection with the actual pharmacological properties of "dangerous drugs." The "danger" of masturbation disappeared when we ceased to believe in it: we then ceased to attribute danger to the practice and to its practitioners; and ceased to call it "self-abuse."

Of course, some people still behave in disagreeable and even dangerous ways, but we no longer attribute their behavior to masturbation or self-abuse: we now attribute their behavior to self-medication or drug abuse. We thus play a game of musical chairs with medical alibis for human desire, determination, and depravity. Though this sort of intolerance is easy, it is also expensive: it seems clear that only in accepting human beings for what they are can we accept the chemical substances they use for what they are. In short, only insofar as we are able and willing to accept men, women, and children as neither angels nor devils, but as persons with certain inalienable rights and irrepudiable duties, shall we be able and willing to accept heroin, cocaine, and marijuana as neither panaceas nor panapathogens, but as drugs with certain chemical properties and ceremonial possibilities.

Notes

[1] *See* Thomas Szasz, *The Second Sin* (Garden City, NY: Doubleday, 1973).
[2] *See, especially,* Ludwig von Mises, *Human Action: A Treatise on Economics* (New Haven: Yale University Press, 1949).
[3] *See, for example,* S. Auerbach, "'Behavior Control' Is Scored," *Miami Herald,* Dec. 28, 1972, p. 15-A.

Chapter Ten

The Scapegoat as Drug
and the Drug as Scapegoat

T housands of years ago—in times we are fond of calling "primitive" (since this renders us "modern" without having to exert
ourselves further to earn this qualification)—religion and
medicine were a united and undifferentiated enterprise; and both were
closely allied with government and politics—all being concerned with
maintaining the integrity of the community and of the individuals who
were its members. How did ancient societies and their priest-physi-
cians protect people from plagues and famines, from the perils of im-
pending military encounters, and from all the other calamities that
threaten persons and peoples? They did so, in general, by performing
certain religious ceremonies.

In ancient Greece (as elsewhere), one of these ceremonies consisted of human sacrifice. The selection, naming, special treatment
and, finally, the ritualized destruction of the scapegoat was the most
important and most potent "therapeutic" intervention known to
"primitive" man. In ancient Greece, the person sacrificed as a scapegoat was called the *pharmakos*. The root of modern terms such as
pharmacology and *pharmacopeia* is therefore not "medicine," "drug,"
and "poison," as most dictionaries erroneously state, but "scapegoat"!
To be sure, after the practice of human sacrifice was abandoned in
Greece, probably around the sixth century B.C., the word did come to
mean "medicine," "drug," and "poison." Interestingly, in modern
Albanian *pharmak* still means only "poison."

The "modern" reader might be tempted to shrug off all this as
etymological curiosity. The magic in which his ancestors believed he

considers "nonsense." He doesn't believe in magic. He "believes" only in facts, in science, in medicine. Insofar as this critical characterization of the modern mind is accurate, it shows us starkly two things: first, that just as human anatomy and physiology have changed little if at all during the past, say, three thousand years, so social organizations and the principles of social control have also changed little if at all; and second, that, in some ways at least, modern man may be more "primitive" than was ancient man. When the ancients saw a scapegoat, they could at least recognize him for what he was: a *pharmakos,* a human sacrifice. When modern man sees one, he does not, or refuses to, recognize him for what he is; instead, he looks for "scientific" explanations—to explain away the obvious. Thus, to the modern mind, the witches were mentally sick women; the Jews in Nazi Germany were the victims of a mass psychosis; involuntary mental patients are sick people unaware of their own need for treatment; and so on. I submit, and will try to show, that among the long list of scapegoats which the insatiable human appetite for *pharmakoi* seems to demand, some of the most important today are certain substances—called "dangerous drugs," "narcotics," or "dope"; certain entrepreneurs—called "pushers" or "drug traffickers"; and certain persons who use certain prohibited substances—called "drug addicts," "drug abusers," or "drug-dependent persons." This pseudoscientific and pseudomedical language is both the cause and the result of the shocking modern insensibility concerning scapegoating and insensitivity toward scapegoats. Civilized man, in contrast to his primitive forebear, "knows" that opium is a dangerous narcotic; that people who sell it are evil individuals, properly analogized with, and treated as, murderers; and that persons who use it are at once sick and sinful, and should be "treated" against their will for their own good—in short, he "knows" that none of them is a scapegoat. Thus, an advertisement for the new 1973 New York state drug law concludes with this revealing plea and promise: "Protect the addicts from themselves and help make New York a better place to live."[1]

The ancient Greeks would have recognized the situation to which this law refers and of which it is itself an important part, as having to do with *pharmakoi,* rather than with pharmacology. We don't. The fact that we don't is a measure of man's irrepressible inhumanity to man, expressed through his unappeasable appetite for human sacrifice. I shall try to show how this appetite is now satisfied through our belief in pharmacomythology and through its characteristic rituals of ceremonial chemistry. To follow my argument, it will be necessary to suspend our faith in conventional wisdom, especially as that wisdom now defines and sees the Church, the State, and Medicine.

The First Amendment to the Constitution of the United States decrees a separation between Church and State, thus implying that they are separate and separable institutions. In a similar way, modern societies distinguish sharply between religion and medicine, clergymen and physicians, implying that the priestly and medical enterprises and institutions are separate and separable. Within certain—quite narrow—limits and for certain—quite discrete—purposes, it is indeed possible and desirable to distinguish religion from medicine, and each from government. However, these distinctions, and the habits of language and mind that they engender, have made us lose sight of some very old, very simple, and very profound truths: in particular, that the most important business of every society is the regulation of the behavior of its members; that there was, in the ancient world, no separation between the roles of priest and physician; and that, in the modern world also, Church, Medicine, and State continue to collaborate in maintaining social order by regulating personal conduct.

The fundamental concept with respect to social control is, of course, "law," which was formerly "rabbinical," "canonical," and "ecclesiastic"—as well as "secular," "political," or "legal"; and which is now ostensibly wholly "secular" or "legal"—while it is actually also "religious" and "political," and most importantly "medical" and "psychiatric." It is impressive testimony to our powers of self-deception that we believe we can expand our civil liberties by opposing threats to it from politicians, while at the same time inviting and embracing threats to it from physicians and psychiatrists.

Illustrative of these threats to our liberties, and of the essential unity of religious, medical, and legal concepts and sanctions in the laws that threaten them, are the new New York state drug laws which became effective on September 1, 1973. In large—nearly full-page—newspaper advertisements warning people: "Don't Get Caught Holding the Bag," the purpose of the new laws is explained as follows: "To deter people from the unlawful sale or possession of illegal drugs and to rehabilitate those people who are, or are in imminent danger of becoming, dependent on these drugs."[2] The idea of "rehabilitating" persons from the "imminent danger of becoming dependent" on drugs which the government of the state of New York does not want them to use is, of course, essentially religious, with respect to both the offense and the sanctions for it.

The amalgamation of medicine, psychiatry, and law, implicit in all such laws, is made fully explicit in the advertisement by the names of the new laws—which are: "Public Health Law: Article 33; Mental Hygiene Law: Article 81; Penal Law: Article 220." We further learn that "the drug laws provide a schedule of crimes ... and related penalties." "Addicts" are then urged to get "treatment": "Besides enforcing the law, the State is spending money for drug abuse treatment.... A treatment program is available 24 hours a day. All you have to do is call!"[3]

The contents of these laws—that is, the behaviors proscribed and the penalties prescribed for them—illustrate, finally, the combined magical, medical, and political character of such legislation. The penalty for the unlawful possession of two ounces or more of "any narcotic substance" is "15 years to life imprisonment"; for the unlawful possession of one ounce or more of marijuana, it is one to fifteen years of imprisonment; and for the unlawful possession of five milligrams or more of LSD, it is one year to life imprisonment.

To understand why some people take certain substances, and why others declare these substances "unlawful" and savagely punish those who take them, we must begin at the beginning, with the basic principles of social congregation and social control.

In her classic study of Greek religion, Jane Ellen Harrison describes what she considers to be a fundamental law of social organization in general and of religious ritual in particular—namely, "the conservation and promotion of life."[4] This protection of the life of both the individual and the community is achieved "in two ways, one negative, one positive, by the riddance of whatever is conceived to be hostile and by the enhancement of whatever is conceived of as favorable to life."[5]

In order that he may live, writes Harrison, "primitive man has before him the old dual task to get rid of evil and secure good. Evil is to him of course mainly hunger and barrenness. Good is food and fertility. The Hebrew word for 'good' meant originally good to eat."[6] Individuals and societies thus seek to include that which they consider good and to exclude that which they consider evil. This principle may also be inverted: individuals or groups may, and often do, promote or prohibit certain substances to justify defining them as good or bad. The ritual thus symbolizes and defines the character of the substance that is ceremonially sought or avoided, and the belief about the goodness or badness of the substance in turn supports the ritual. This explains the social stability of such beliefs and rituals and their relative immunity to "rational" or "scientific" arguments seeking to alter them. It also explains why some individuals and groups are as deeply committed to the (ritual) use of certain substances—such as alcohol or opium, beef or pork—as others are to their (ritual) avoidance.

The ceremonial of the scapegoat is surely one of the most important instances and prototypes of all riddance rituals. In Greece during the first century A.D., the scapegoat was not killed but only ritually expelled. The ceremony was described by Plutarch (c. 46–120), who, as chief magistrate of his native town, himself performed the ceremony, playing the role, of course, of the scapegoater. Harrison describes the ceremony as follows: "The little township of Chaeronea in Boeotia, Plutarch's birthplace, saw enacted year by year a strange and very ancient ceremonial. It was called 'The Driving out of the Famine.' A household slave was driven out of doors with rods of *agnus castus,* a willowlike plant, and over him were pronounced the words, 'Out with Famine, in with Health and Wealth.'"[7]

While this was merely a mock sacrifice of the scapegoat, there were actual scapegoat sacrifices in Greece, both before Plutarch's time and after it. At one time, Frazer tells us, the Athenians maintained "a number of degraded and useless beings at public expense; and when any calamity ... befell the city, they sacrificed two of these outcast scapegoats."[8] Moreover, such sacrifices were not confined to extraordinary occasions but were regular religious ceremonials. Every year, Frazer writes, "at the festival of the Thargelia in May, two victims, one for the men and one for the women, were led out of Athens and stoned to death. The city of Abdera in Thrace was publicly purified once a year, and one of the burghers, set apart for the purpose, was stoned to death as a scapegoat or vicarious sacrifice for the life of all the others...."[9]

As I have mentioned earlier, the Greek name for persons so sacrificed was *pharmakoi.* John Cuthbert Lawson's account of this ritual human sacrifice is instructive in this connection: "If calamity overtook the city through divine wrath, whether it were famine or pestilence or any other bane, a *pharmakos* was led out to an appointed place for sacrifice. Cheese, barley-cake, and dried figs were given to him. He was smitten seven times on the privy parts with squills and wild figs and other wild plants; and finally he was burnt with fire upon fuel collected from wild trees, and the ashes were scattered to the winds and the sea."[10]

This sort of explicit destruction of human scapegoats is distasteful to the more "civilized" or "modern" mentality, which prefers to disguise its ceremonials of scapegoating. For example, Gilbert Murray observes: "The memory of a time when human beings had been deliberately slaughtered as a way of pleasing God runs through the literature of the fifth century as of something far-off, romantic, horrible. We may compare it to our own memories of the burning of heretics and witches, deeds which we know to have been done quite lately, by men very like ourselves, and yet deeds which we can scarcely conceive as psychologically possible to any sane being. In just the same way, to the earliest of the great Athenians, Aeschylus, the sacrifice of Iphigenia is something monstrous, beyond understanding. The man who did it must have been mad. To Euripides such acts are generally connected with a study of the worst possibilities of the savage mob, or of scheming kings led by malignant and half-insane priests."[11]

It is significant, then, how deeply pervasive the human passion is not only for victimizing scapegoats but also for trying to conceal this passion by attributing it to madness.

According to Murray, the word *pharmakos* "means literally 'human medicines' or 'scapegoats.'"[12] Martin Nilsson offers a similar but even more telling interpretation of it. The *pharmakoi*, he asserts, were "like a sponge with which one dries a table [who] when they have absorbed all the impurity, are entirely destroyed so that this impurity shall be altogether removed with them; they are thrown away, burnt up, cast into the sea. And that is why this 'sacrifice,' so-called, need not, like others, be without blemish or defect. A dog may be used, which was otherwise never sacrificed, or a condemned criminal. He was called *pharmakos*, 'remedy,' *peripsema*, 'off-scouring,' or *katharmada*, 'that which is wiped off'; this last word in particular clearly shows the meaning of the rite. We can understand how these words came to mean 'scum' and became the worst terms of abuse in the Greek language. A victim of this nature is a scapegoat upon which all evil is loaded, but which, instead of being let loose and driven into the desert, is completely destroyed, together with its evil burden."[13]

The similarities between this imagery and that conjured up by the burning of heretics, witches, Jews, and prohibited books and drugs are arresting and significant. And so are also the similarities between the later mitigated ceremonials of the *pharmakos* and the contemporary mitigated ceremonial incarcerations, rather than incinerations, of madmen and drug abusers.

For an account of a modified scapegoat ceremonial, Murray refers to Ister, a third-century historian, who gave this account of the ritual: "Two persons, one for the men of the city, one for the women, were led out as though to execution. They wore necklaces, one of white figs, the other of black. They seem to have been solemnly presented with cake and figs and then scourged and pelted out of the city.... At the end, the *pharmakoi* were supposed to be dead and their ashes were thrown into the sea. The ceremony was an 'imitation,' says Ister, of a stoning to death.'"[14]

Murray is not impressed by this disclaimer and cites instances of human sacrifice which contradict Ister. He is, indeed, fully aware of the depth of the human passion for scapegoating, so easily mobilized in times of public anguish and distress. "As a matter of fact," adds Murray, "it is just on occasions like this that human sacrifices have most tended to occur: in a disorganized army or a rabble full of fear, egged on by some fanatical priest or prophet. There were bloody doings in Rome when the fear of Hannibal was strong, judicial murders of vestal virgins, burying alive of 'Gallus et Galla, Graecus et Graeca' in the Forum Boarium."[15]

By the early 1960s, a generation after triumphing over all their enemies in the Second World War, the American people were also full of fears and were egged on by fanatical priests of drug-abuseology. The result was the invention of a new imagery of pollution—by drugs, drug pushers, and drug addicts; and of a correspondingly new category of *pharmakoi*—whose burden of evil is, literally, pharmacological.

To be sure, there is an important difference between the ancient Greek *pharmakos* and the modern American pharmacological scapegoat. The former, an expendable person, was an object or thing: he or she was an effigy or symbol—the scapegoat—in a purification ceremony. The latter (when an individual rather than a drug), although still an expendable person, is both object and subject, thing and agent: he or she is an effigy or symbol—the scapegoat—in a purification ceremony; and also a participant—the addict or pusher—in a counter-ceremony celebrating a substance tabooed by society's dominant ethic.

Many of the most dramatic moments of history, both biblical and secular, have to do with *pharmakoi*. According to Paton, Adam and Eve were *pharmakoi*,[16] an interpretation that would make God the first scapegoater. Certainly, the legend is consistent with God's need to purify His Garden, polluted by Man's ingestion of a forbidden substance. All men and women are thus scapegoats. When they reject this role, they often do so by becoming scapegoaters.

Abraham's near-sacrifice of his son transforms Isaac into still another *pharmakos* and supports the imagery of the Jewish God as a scapegoater. The self-definition of the Jews as God's Chosen People may thus be viewed as their attempt to escape from the role of scapegoat by casting all non-Jews into that role through their implicit status as God's stepchildren or castoffs.

That the central figure in the Christian religions is a *pharmakos* is obvious. Christ, moreover, was a great healer even while "alive." Resurrected as a deity, He is truly the Christian *panacea*, the cure-all for all ills, a function previously discharged, as we have seen, through the ceremonial killing of the *pharmakos*.

Thus we come full circle: from *pharmakoi* to pharmacology; from cure-alls through human sacrifice to cure-alls through chemistry; and to the sacrifice of pharmacological *pharmakoi*—through whose expulsion Man, the god of chemistry, seeks to purify his polluted earthly Garden.

Notes

[1]"How the New Drug Laws Affect You," *Syracuse Post-Standard,* Aug. 20, 1973, p. 5.
[2]Ibid.
[3]Ibid.
[4]Jane Ellen Harrison, *Epilegomena to the Study of Greek Religion and Themis: A Study of the Social Origins of Greek Religion* [1912, 1921], (New Hyde Park, NY: University Books, 1962), p. xvii.
[5]Ibid.
[6]Ibid.
[7]Ibid.
[8]James George Frazer, *The Golden Bough: A Study in Magic and Religion* [1922], abridged ed. (New York: Macmillan, 1942), p. 579.
[9]Ibid.
[10]John Cuthbert Lawson, *Modern Greek Folklore and Ancient Greek Religion:*

A Study of Survivals, (Cambridge, England: Cambridge University Press, 1910), p. 355.

[11]Gilbert Murray, *The Rise of the Greek Epic,* 3d ed. (Oxford: Clarendon Press, 1924), pp. 11–12.

[12]Ibid., p. 12.

[13]Martin P. Nilsson, *A History of Greek Religion,* trans. by F.J. Fielden (Oxford: Clarendon Press, 1925), p. 87.

[14]Murray, op. cit., pp. 12–13.

[15]Ibid., p. 14.

[16]W.R. Paton, "The *Pharmakoi* and the Story of the Fall," *Revue Archéologique,* 3:51–57, 1907.

TABLE 1

THE THEOCRATIC AND THERAPEUTIC PERSPECTIVES IN SUMMARY

	Theocratic State	Therapeutic State
Dominant ideology	Religious/Christian	Scientific/medical
Dominant value	Grace	Health
Interpreters, justifiers, prescribers, and proscribers of conduct and their ostensible aim	Priests Clerics Nuns Saving souls	Physicians Clinicians Nurses Curing bodies and minds
Heroes	Saints	Heroic healers
Heretics	Witches	Quacks
Ceremonies and Rituals	Baptism Holy Eucharist Confession, penance Holy Orders Holy Matrimony Miracles Exorcism Extreme Unction	Medical birth certification Psychopharmacology Psychotherapy M.D. degree Psychiatry as medical specialty Transplants Electroshock, lobotomy Medical death certification
Panaceas	Faith Hope Charity Holy water	Scientific knowledge Scientific research Compulsory treatment Therapeutic drugs
Panapathogens	Satan Blasphemy Witch's brew Jews and Jewish poisoners	Christian Scientists and others who defy the authority of medicine Rejection of medical science and medical treatment "Dangerous drugs" Drug addicts and pushers
Prohibited objects	The Bible in the "vulgar" tongue "Dangerous books" (Index of prohibited books)	Drugs in the free market "Dangerous drugs" (Index of prohibited drugs)
Unprofessional conduct	Selling too many indulgences Questioning the infallibility of the Mother Church	Writing too many prescriptions for "dangerous drugs" Questioning the infallibility of modern medicine
Agency of social sanction	The Inquisition	Institutional psychiatry
Aim of social sanction	Forced religious conversion	Forced psychiatric personality change
Intended domain or sphere of influence	The world	The world

Chapter Eleven

Cures and Controls: Panaceas and Panapathogens

Because one of the dominant passions of human beings is to control—themselves, other persons, and natural events—all cultures develop systems of explanations that function both as accounts of why good and bad things happen and as methods for causing them to happen. Magic and religion are, of course, the oldest and most familiar systems of such explanations and methods of control; or, more precisely, today, when we believe in science as an explanation and method of controlling persons and things, we call former beliefs and practices, in which we no longer believe, magical and religious.

In what follows, I shall not be concerned with the empirical validity of the claims attributed to the various "explanations" and "causes," as I shall consider only such extensions of them into explain-alls and cause-alls which are, at least to those who are not true believers in them, patently false. Indeed, the very concept of panacea implies such exaggerated powers—resembling powers that religions attribute to deities—as to engender doubt as well as faith. The *Oxford English Dictionary* defines a panacea as "a remedy, cure, or medicine, reputed to heal all diseases"; and it offers such examples of its use as the following: "Phlebotomie, which is their panacea for all diseases (1652)"; and "Coffee was his panacea (1867)."

The magical or religious character of panaceas—and of their opposites, which I shall call "panapathogens"—is also revealed by the role they have played and continue to play in the history of medicine. Simply put, these two categories of agents—formerly theological but now

Chapter 10 from *Ceremonial Chemistry: The Ritual Persecution of Drugs, Addicts, and Pushers* is reprinted with permission of Learning Publications, Inc. Copyright 1985 by Thomas S. Szasz. All rights reserved.

therapeutic in character—are the saviors and scapegoats of society; they constitute the ceremonial symbols for the collectivity's rituals of purification and pollution.[1] (For a list of the principal panaceas and panapathogens in the history of the Western world, see Table 2.)

Medicine has a dual social character and function: to cure disease and to control deviance. For far too long, however, the doctor's role as priest or policeman has been subsumed under, and disguised as, his role as physician—with the unfortunate result that the relief of pain has become commingled and confused with the repression of protest, both being called simply "treatment."

I believe the time is ripe now for pinpointing the differences between these two radically disparate medical functions; that is, for identifying, accurately and honestly, the mechanisms—linguistic, legal, moral, and technical—by means of which the medical profession, at

TABLE 2
THE PRINCIPAL PANACEAS AND PANAPATHOGENS
IN THE HISTORY OF THE WESTERN WORLD

Period or World View	Panacea	Panapathogen
1. Christianity	God Baptism Jesus Imitation Faith Prayer Misery Benediction Resurrection Sacraments Holy water	Satan Original sin Jews Originality Skepticism Blasphemy Pleasure Malediction Insurrection Sacrilege Witch's brew
2. Enlightenment	Knowledge Science	Ignorance Superstition
3. 18th and 19th century medicine	Opium	Masturbation
4. Individualism	Freedom and responsibility	Determinism and planning
5. Collectivism	The state	The individual
6. Modern scientific-statist world view	Internationalism Science Research Innovation Physician	Nationalism Magic Religion Tradition Quack
7. Pharmacracy	Legitimate, "holy" drugs	Illegitimate, "unholy" drugs

the behest of both the state and its own ambitions for power, exercises social control over personal conduct.

Inasmuch as we have words to describe medicine as a healing art, but have none to describe it as a method of social control or political rule, we must first give it a name. I propose that we call it *pharmacracy,* from the Greek roots *pharmakon,* for "medicine" or "drug," and *kratein,* for "to rule" or "to control." Pharmacology is the science of drugs and, especially, of the therapeutic and toxic effects and uses of drugs. It is appropriate, then, that a system of political controls based on and exercised in the name of drugs should be called a "pharmacracy." As theocracy is rule by God or priests, and democracy is rule by the people or the majority, so pharmacracy is rule by medicine or physicians.

In the sense in which I propose to use this term, pharmacracy is the characteristic technical form of that particular modern sociopolitical organization which more than a decade ago I named the "Therapeutic State."[2] Contemporary pharmacracies rule mainly by means of drug controls—a rule aptly symbolized by the linguistic and legal powers of the physician's "prescription." Their rule is of relatively recent origin: it is sometime during the nineteenth century somewhere in western Europe—I have been unable to ascertain the exact time and place—that, for the first time in human history, the law distinguishes between ordinary citizen on the one hand and physician and pharmacist on the other, prohibiting the former from free access to certain "drugs," reserving such access, for the purpose of providing "treatment," to the latter.[3] We have since witnessed the steady growth of the powers of pharmacracy. Today especially in the United States, its rule is absolute and capricious—that is, tyrannical. Although pharmacracies now rule mainly by means of drug controls and psychiatric controls—that is, by using medical justifications and personnel for repressing "dangerous drugs" and "dangerous mental patients"—it is quite possible that as these methods are publicly exposed and thus rendered morally distasteful, the technology of pharmacratic repression may shift to behavior modification and psychosurgery.

In the modern Western therapeutic societies, the political and medical decision makers control the definition of drugs as therapeutic or toxic, and hence also their legitimacy and availability in the marketplace. The definitions of tobacco and alcohol as agricultural products and of marijuana and opium as dangerous drugs—definitions authen-

ticated by both the United States government and the United Nations—at once illustrate that we live in a pharmacracy and display its
particular values.

The difference between pharmacology and pharmacracy—that is,
between science as a body of facts and theories and scientism as a
system of justifications for social policy and social control—is illus-
trated by the following typical account from the daily press. In an
Associated Press report entitled "Saccharin Suspect in Study," the
American people were informed—in the first sentence of the story—
that "a new federal report shows 'presumptive evidence' that saccharin
in high doses causes cancerous bladder tumors in rats."[4] What those
who read the rest of the story discovered was that forty-eight rats were
fed saccharin as 7.5 percent of their total diet and that three of these
rats developed tumors that "may be" cancerous. Nowhere in the
newspaper report, running to some three hundred words, was there
even the merest hint that rats fed, for example, sodium chloride—that
is, table salt—as 7.5 percent of their total diet might not remain very
healthy either. Instead, the reader was told, in tones of high solemnity,
that "the Food and Drug Administration said it will not move against
saccharin, the only artificial sweetener remaining on the market since
cyclamate was banned, until it received a recommendation from the
National Academy of Sciences."[5]

When cigarettes were discovered to be toxic—something that had
been known for decades before the "discovery" became officially recognized by the United States government—they were labeled as "dangerous to health." When cyclamate was discovered to be toxic—a
claim whose validity, in cases where the substance is used in low doses,
remains in serious doubt—it was banned entirely: pharmaceutical
companies are enjoined from manufacturing it and people cannot buy
it. Similarly, in the report cited above, the public is not told that,
should saccharin prove to be potentially toxic, it would be so labeled;
instead, it is told that, if the National Academy of Sciences "recom-
mends" banning saccharin, then the government will ban it. That is
pharmacracy in action.

Ostensibly, "therapeutic" panaceas are agents of medical cure;
actually, they are—just as are those that are overtly religious—agents
of magical control. A brief review of some of the major "therapeutic"
panaceas of the past two thousand years will support this interpretation
and show how remarkably similar the claims for these various agents

actually are.

Galen (130–c. 200) was the founder of the most important school of medicine of his age, a school whose influence extended through the Middle Ages. In Galenic practice the most useful medicine was a *theriaca*, or antidote, named *Electuarium theriacale magnum*, a compound composed of several ingredients, among them opium and wine. Its powers, according to Galen, were as follows: "It resists poison and venomous bites, cures inveterate headache, vertigo, deafness, epilepsy, apoplexy, dimness of sight, loss of voice, asthma, coughs of all kinds, spitting of blood, tightness of breath, colic, the iliac poison, jaundice, hardness of the spleen, stone, urinary complaints, fevers, dropsies, leprosies, the troubles to which women are subject, melancholy, and all pestilences."[6]

Although opium remained a medical panacea until the end of the nineteenth century, from the Middle Ages on similar claims were made for other substances as well, especially for alcohol. Here is a thirteenth-century account of the beneficent powers of alcohol— which, of course, used to be called *aqua vitae*, the water of life:

> It sloweth age, it strengtheneth youth, it helpeth digestion, it abandoneth melancholie, it relisheth the heart, it lighteneth the mind, it quickeneth the spirit, it keepeth and preserveth the head from whirling, the eyes from dazzling, the tongue from lisping, the mouth from snaffling, the teeth from chattering, and the throat from rattling; it keepeth the stomach from wambling, the heart from swelling, the hands from shivering, the sinews from shrinking, the veins from crumbling, the bones from aching, and the marrow from soaking.[7]

In China, the medical panacea was tea. The following is a description of tea sold in Canton in the second half of the nineteenth century:

> The never-failing Midday Tea; its taste and odour are pure and fragrant, its qualities temperate and mild.... The stomach is strengthened by its use; it creates appetite, dissolves secretions, assuages the most burning thirst, checks colds, dispels vapours; in a word, the inner distempers and outer complaints are all allayed by this tea. Is it not divine? ... The medicinal herbs of which it is composed are culled with the nicest attention.... It is dared to be

publicly asserted, that although it may not always be *positively* beneficial in illness, yet in respect to longevity it will be found wonderful.[8]

The language in which the claims for the evil effects of panapathogens are cast, and the imagery they conjure up, parallels the language and imagery of panaceas. Until the Renaissance the leading Western panapathogens were the devil, witches, and Jews. Since then, they have been madness, masturbation and, most recently, dangerous drugs, addicts, and pushers.

The transformation of panaceas into panapathogens is both a cause and a consequence of the ideological transformation that it expresses. Although seemingly a radical change, such a transformation is often no more than a change in ceremonial symbols, leaving the basic fabric of social organization and control largely unaltered. For example, with the change in Russia from Czarism to Communism, the religious panaceas of Christianity became panapathogens; the oligarchic, tyrannical nature of Russian rule, however, remained the same. Similarly, with the change in medical sexology from Krafft-Ebing and Freud to Masters and Johnson, masturbation was transformed from panapathogen into panacea; the paternalistic rule of doctors over patients, however, remained the same.

This metamorphosis—for which the degradation of opium and cocaine are our best examples—progresses through a definite pattern of discrete phases. First, the substance—let us call it X—is freely available. As the rulers realize that, although X is not required for survival, people want it and will pay money for it, they seize upon it as a source of revenue: the government now imposes a tax on X, subjecting it to economic regulation. Next, X is defined as a drug, making its use legitimate only for the treatment of illness: the government, with the zealous support of the medical profession, now restricts its use to prescription by a physician, subjecting X to medical controls. This creates both a black market in X and "abuses" in its medical distribution through physicians' "overprescriptions," setting the stage for political and popular demand for more stringent controls over X. Finally, to justify and facilitate total prohibition, "medical research" reveals that there are no "legitimate therapeutic" indications or uses for X at all: since any and all use of X is now viewed as "abuse," politicians, physicians, and the people unite in banning X altogether.

We have actually lived through this pattern of escalating prohibition—transforming a freely available useful substance into the strictly prohibited scourge of mankind—with both opium and cocaine. We have lived through some of its phases, without carrying the process to completion, with alcohol, tobacco, amphetamines, vitamins A and D in large doses, and other substances. It seems safe to predict that in the near future we are likely to see other substances—perhaps aspirin, saccharin, and who knows what else—subjected to such pharmacratic controls. To help appreciate the influence of permissions, prescriptions, and prohibitions on our ideas about drugs and their uses, I have constructed, in Table 3, a classification of drugs—not, as is customary, in terms of their pharmacological actions, but in terms of their availability, distribution, and use.

Just as the human impulses to cure and to control are at once complementary and contradictory, so too are the principles of pharmacology and pharmacracy. I have indicated this relationship between them in Table 4. The idea of control is an all-inclusive concept, subsuming the notion of cure. Treatment, as we usually conceive of it, is a non-coercive type of social control, relying for its effect wholly on the initiative and cooperation of the sick person. Whereas contemporary drug laws (and mental hygiene and public health laws) are coercive types of social controls, relying for their effects on the police powers of the state. This interpretation is consistent with all our historical experience with medicine as a healing art.

Before the second half of the nineteenth century, when modern therapeutic medicine as we now know it took its first stumbling steps, there was virtually nothing that physicians could do to alleviate disease. And the less effective were their remedies, the more plentiful were their panaceas: besides opium and alcohol, phlebotomy (bloodletting), purgation with calomel (mercurous chloride), blistering, and a host of other things that physicians gave to patients or did to them were all regarded, at one time or another, as cure-alls. Since the development of effective therapeutic agents and measures, especially during the past few decades, medical scientists and physicians have learned that every chemical and physical intervention in the human organism produces certain clear-cut consequences in it. Instead of panaceas or general remedies, physicians now speak of specific measures, useful for one or at most a few conditions, but useless or harmful for others. Penicillin is therapeutic for some infections, but not for others; an appendectomy

TABLE 3

A CLASSIFICATION OF DRUGS BY MODE OF AVAILABILITY, DISTRIBUTION, AND USE

Class of Drug	Exemplifying Members of the Class	Expected Use
I. Non-medical drugs ("Non-drugs")		
1. Foods	Sugar, carbohydrates, fats, and proteins	As part of "normal" diet
2. Substances added to foods	Salt, condiments and spices, food colorings, preservatives, other chemicals	As part of "normal" process of eating commercially merchandised foods
3. Beverages	Water, coffee, tea, cocoa, etc.	As part of "normal" diet
4. Substances added to water	Chlorine, fluorides, and other chemicals	As part of "normal" process of drinking "medically safe" water
5. Substances applied to the body	Cosmetics, perfumes, antiperspirants, etc.	As part of "normal" process of beautifying the body
6. Body cleansers	Soap, toothpaste, mouth-wash, douches, etc.	As part of "normal" process of cleaning the body
7. Socially acceptable recreational substances	Alcohol, nicotine, caffeine	At all socially appropriate occasions and times
8. Substances used in the home, industry, transportation, etc.	Gasoline, detergents, lye, glue, paint, varnish, pesticides, furniture polish, etc.	As part of "normal" process of homemaking, farming, manufacturing, traveling, etc.
II. Medical drugs ("Therapeutic drugs")		
9. Over-the-counter drugs	Antacids Anti-cold medicines Aspirin Laxatives Vitamins	If slightly ill (diagnosed by self)
10. Prescription drugs	Insulin Morphine Penicillin	If seriously ill (diagnosed by physician)
11. Drugs restricted to special medical personnel and settings	Antabuse Methadone	If "specially" ill ("addict")
III. Illegal drugs		
12. Disapproved therapeutic drugs	Thalidomide	None
13. Disapproved food and beverage additives or substitutes	Cyclamates	None
14. Disapproved recreational drugs	Heroin Cocaine Marijuana	If member of counter-culture (if desires to defy the "establishment")

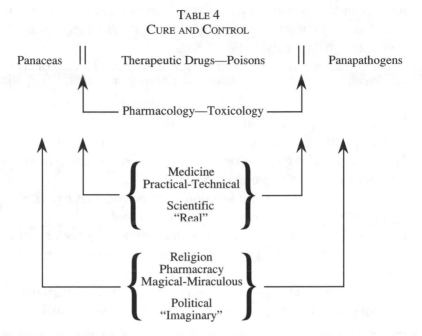

TABLE 4
CURE AND CONTROL

Panaceas ‖ Therapeutic Drugs—Poisons ‖ Panapathogens

Pharmacology—Toxicology

{ Medicine
Practical-Technical

Scientific
"Real" }

{ Religion
Pharmacracy
Magical-Miraculous }

Political
"Imaginary"

is therapeutic only for an acutely inflamed appendix; and so forth. In contrast, such modern "medical treatments" as Christian Science, psychoanalysis, the mud and waters of spas, vegetarianism, and vitamin C reveal their characters as panaceas through their alleged powers to prevent and cure an almost endless variety of ailments.

All this is consistent with the fact that insofar as the physician's work remains a combination of applied science and medical magic, people continue to seek medical help for problems in the face of which physicians are as helpless today as were their predecessors in the face of the plagues. Some of these problems pertain to diseases, such as cancer and the so-called degenerative diseases; others do not pertain to genuine diseases at all, such as the countless difficulties of everyday living now called "mental illness." When confronted with these, physicians continue to offer panaceas; and patients, ever credulous and submissive, continue to accept and, indeed, to demand them. In our day, the most obvious panaceas are diets and tranquilizing drugs. Moreover, as in former religious ages when the cure-alls and cause-alls were theological in character, so in our age the cure-alls and cause-alls are medical in character. This age was ushered in, as I have shown elsewhere,[9] by the "discovery" of two medical cause-alls of all human problems:

insanity and masturbation; while the former explained why men engaged in every conceivable form of mischief, the latter explained why they contracted insanity!

Although it is now nearly three hundred years old, the concept of mental illness—as a panchreston (explain-all) and panapathogen—has reached its full flowering only in our day; with its efflorescence, there have emerged special instances or members of it, such as drug abuse and drug addiction—the causes and symptoms of mental illness in the Free Societies; and religious observances—the causes and symptoms of mental illness in the Communist Societies.

To be sure, the Communists don't like narcotics either. They are against all sorts of things which express or symbolize the autonomy of the individual. My point, however, is that just as our principal panapathogen now is the Dangerous Drug, the Communists' is the Dangerous Religion. If this parallel—and more specifically, the parallel between heroin and holy water—seems exaggerated, perhaps the following report, distributed by the Associated Press, will make it seem less so.

On March 27, 1973, "an Austrian Catholic news service reported that a priest, identified as Stephan Kurti, had been executed in Albania, condemned to death for secretly baptizing a child."[10] Evidently, to the Albanians, Kurti is a "pusher" of holy water who deserves to die, just as to many Americans, importers of heroin are "pushers" who also deserve to die.

Moreover, just as the Capitalist Crusade is aimed not only against heroin but against all "dangerous drugs," so the Communist Crusade is aimed not only against holy water but against all religions.

From the same Associated Press report we learn that, on March 31, 1973, the Vatican radio announced that Communist Albania "'has suffocated all forms of Christian life in its plan aimed at the total destruction of the Roman Catholic Church…. There are no religious buildings…. They have all been transformed into dance halls, gymnasiums, or government offices…. The Orthodox churches and the Moslem mosques had the same fate.'"[11]

This is not an isolated report. Other Communist authorities on mental health have long claimed that religion causes countless mental diseases and social disorders, a claim identical to that which American mental health experts make about "dangerous drugs." For example, according to a 1972 Associated Press news report from Prague, the

Slovak Communist party organ *Pravda* has warned "Czechoslovak parents ... that religion constitutes a grave hazard for the mental health of children. Religion interferes with sound and harmonious emotional development ... it impedes social adaptability, creating the conditions for the emergence of delinquency. By burdening the nervous system, it leads to psychical disorders. It brings up individuals with an undermined will and stands in the way of the development of firm moral sentiments.... It weakens the will to learn, leading to lower grades."[12]

This Communist image of religion as panapathogen is just as much a part of their customs and laws as our image is concerning drugs: we warn travelers not to bring narcotics into the United States; the Russians warn travelers not to bring Bibles into the U.S.S.R.[13]

These examples amply demonstrate that the differences between pharmacology and pharmacracy are, in the last analysis, the same as the differences between description and prescription, fact and value, medicine and morals. In short, panaceas and panapathogens are counters in a calculus of justificatory rhetoric: they do not assert facts, but justify—nay, incite to—actions.

Although ostensibly aimed at protecting the layman, pharmacratic controls ultimately injure both patient and physician. The citizen as potential sick person is injured because he is deprived of the right to self-medication; of the opportunity and right to select the expert of his choice—some experts being declared unlicensed and thus prevented by law from offering their services; and of the right to treatment with certain drugs which, although available in other countries, may be forbidden in the United States, even through prescription by accredited physicians.[14]

The physician, favored in the short run by such controls as the beneficiary of a government-protected monopoly, is ultimately also victimized, mainly as a result of the enforcement of precisely those drug controls whose ostensible aim was only the protection of uninformed laymen from "using the wrong medicine." This seemingly altruistic motive and practical goal conceals the drive for domination—of patient by physician, of some physicians by others, of physician by politician—in an unending spiral of regulations and tyrannizations.

The upshot is that the physician is no longer free to prescribe the drug he believes would most benefit his patient, as he was twenty or fifty years ago. First, because he fears that if he prescribes certain drugs, especially psychoactive drugs, "too often" or in quantities considered to be "excessive"—so judged by committees of his peers—he may be punished by sanctions ranging from reprimands to loss of his license to practice medicine.[15] Further, because he fears that since copies of his prescription of "controlled substances" go on file in centralized, politicized registries, these records might later be used to injure his patient—legally, economically, occupationally, or in ways now impossible to anticipate.[16] Lastly, because he fears—or ought to fear—that the person seeking his help is not a patient at all, but an *agent provocateur*. I refer here to an aspect of the war on drugs that has been completely concealed from the public and hence deserves more detailed comment.

Judging by the citation of legal decisions, it has evidently been common law enforcement practice in recent years to deploy undercover narcotics agents posing as patients to doctors' offices, to entrap physicians into prescribing "controlled substances" illegally. Here are the summaries of two such cases, culled from the American Medical Association's periodical abstract of judicial decisions.

In the first case, "an undercover agent assigned to conduct an investigation of illegal narcotic traffic went to the physician's office posing as a patient. He told the physician he was suffering from the aftereffects of taking mescaline and that he was nervous and having trouble sleeping."[17] Perhaps medical schools and textbooks should expand the scope of their instruction: they teach the student about "addicts" and "malingerers," but do not teach him about *agents provocateurs*—now called "narcotics agents" who "pose as patients," fake symptoms and diseases, and seek to entrap the physician into prescribing or dispensing drugs illegally.

The physician in the above case gave the "patient" some barbiturate pills. "The agent returned to the physician's office five more times, requesting prescriptions...." Each time, the physician, a woman, complied—with the result that she "was found guilty of 13 indictments charging violations of various narcotic drug statutes and regulations." In court, the physician argued the defense of entrapment, but the jury ruled against her. She appealed, contending that "it had not been proved beyond a reasonable doubt that she did not act in good faith and that the amount of drugs dispensed was excessive.... The court said the evidence was sufficient to warrant the jury's conclusion that the physician did not act in good faith and that dispensing to the agent of any quantity of drugs or narcotics was excessive and impelled by no legitimate medical purpose. The court said the jury could reach its conclusions from the physician's conduct and testimony, unassisted by expert testimony."[18]

The story speaks for itself. I want to note only that what is a "legitimate medical purpose" for prescribing narcotics was here determined by a jury of non-physicians. The physicians who have so zealously supported the war on "dangerous drugs" no doubt never anticipated that this would be one of its consequences.

In another case, a special agent of the Bureau of Narcotics and Dangerous Drugs "visited a physician in his office and complained of a persistent backache. Without conducting a physical examination, the physician prescribed Parafon Forte."[19] After more compromising behavior with this agent, a second agent was deployed to entrap the doctor. This pseudo-patient "complained of nervousness and inability to sleep." The physician "prescribed Librium, again without conducting a physical examination." This agent also returned for subsequent visits and obtained more drugs. The physician was convicted "on two counts of improperly prescribing controlled drugs to agents of the Federal Bureau of Narcotics and Dangerous Drugs." His conviction was affirmed by a federal appellate court.[20]

This account also speaks for itself. Here I would like to add, however, that psychiatrists regularly prescribe "controlled substances" to patients they do not physically examine. In fact, many psychiatrists believe that it is improper for a physician to examine physically a patient whom he is "treating" by psychotherapy; yet many of these psychiatrists prescribe drugs for their patients. Is the conduct of all of these physicians in violation of the rules and regulations of the Federal Bureau of Narcotics and Dangerous Drugs?

The Harrison Act, passed in 1914, aimed ostensibly at controlling addicts, was actually used to control physicians. That act, it should be recalled, criminalized the free, over-the-counter sale of opium and its derivatives, and made these drugs legally available only through a physician's prescription for the treatment of disease. In a series of Supreme Court decisions following the passage of the act, the Court declared that dispensing or prescribing opiates to addicts is outside the scope of legitimate medical practice and therefore also illegal. According to a study sponsored by the New York Academy of Medicine, in the years following the passage of the Harrison Act, and especially after 1919, 25,000 physicians were arraigned on charges of selling narcotics, and 3,000 actually served prison sentences. Thousands more had their licenses revoked.[21] The handwriting was on the wall, but the American medical profession stubbornly refused to read it.

I have discussed elsewhere the grievous violations committed by physicians against the freedom and dignity of so-called mental patients; in those cases, the protections of the rule of law of a free society are abandoned in favor of the madness controls promised by a tyrannous pharmacracy. Here I want to expose and denounce the grievous violations committed by politicians, legislators, and jurists against the freedom and dignity of physicians; in these cases, the protections of the rule of law of a free society are abandoned in favor of the drug controls promised by a tyrannous pharmacracy.

Threatened with plagues and famines, the medieval European set out to solve his problems by persecuting witches and Jews. Threatened with imperialistic Communism, a shortage of energy, and environmental pollution, the modern American sets out to solve his problems by persecuting marijuana smokers and heroin sellers.

In the American temper, moreover, the panapathogen must not only be combated in action but, perhaps more importantly, must also be legislated out of existence. In 1971, in the Commonwealth of Massachusetts alone, some 143 bills relating to drugs have been introduced. One of these provides for the death penalty "for the possession of with intent to sell narcotic drugs." If all these bills were passed, notes the *Massachusetts Physician,* "a person carrying aspirin tablets might be in jeopardy."[22]

It is indeed tragic that physicians, and people generally, should remain so blind to the wisdom of the Gospels and delude themselves that they can ignore with impunity Jesus' warning that "... all who take the sword shall perish by the sword";[23] that, in other words, all who plan, promote, and profit from drug controls shall perish from drug controls.

Such a warning as this comes, of course, too late to save "free" American medicine from the government controls that threaten it, as American medicine has for too long been a government monopoly rather than a free profession. However, my adaptation, to the requirements of the contemporary drug scene, of a time-honored wisdom from the Gospels makes a fitting epitaph for the headstone of a Medicine devoted to curing the sick but murdered by a brother devoted to controlling the sinful.

Notes

[1] *See* Chapter 10, "The Scapegoat as Drug and the Drug as Scapegoat."

[2] Thomas Szasz, *Law, Liberty, and Psychiatry: An Inquiry into the Social Uses of Mental Health Practices* (New York: Macmillan, 1963), p. 212.

[3] In this connection, *see* David F. Musto, *The American Disease: Origins of Narcotic Control* (New Haven: Yale University Press, 1973).

[4] "Saccharin suspect in study," *The Evening Star and Daily News* (Washington), May 23, 1973, C-back page.

[5] Ibid.

[6] *Quoted in* David I. Macht, "The history of opium and some of its preparations and alkaloids," *Journal of the American Medical Association,* 64:477–481 (Feb. 6), 1915, p. 479.

[7] *Quoted in* Joseph Lyons, *Experience: An Introduction to Personal Psychology,* (New York: Harper & Row, 1973), p. 136.

[8] *Quoted in* William C. Hunter, *Bits of Old China* [1885] (London: Keegan Paul, Trench & Co., 1985), pp. 170–171.

[9] *See* Thomas Szasz, *The Manufacture of Madness: A Comparative Study of the Inquisition and the Mental Health Movement* (New York: Harper & Row, 1970), especially Chapters 9 and 11.

[10] "Atheistic Albania 'suffocates' all religious forms," *San Juan Star* (Puerto Rico), April 1, 1973, p. 10.

[11] Ibid.

[12] "Czechs told religion bad for children," *Syracuse Post-Standard,* Feb. 21, 1972, p. 2.

[13] "This week," *National Review,* Aug. 31, 1973, p. 926.

[14] *See* John Carlova, "Are useful new drugs being bottled up by bureaucracy?" *Medical Economics,* Aug. 6, 1973, pp. 94–106.

[15] *See* Nancy Martin, "Will they challenge your prescribing habits?" *Medical Economics,* Aug. 20, 1973, pp. 31–38.

[16] *See* David A. Green, "The New York tax on prescriptions," *Physician's Management,* 13:15–17 (June) 1973.

[17] *Commonwealth of Massachusetts v. Miller* (1972), quoted in *The Citation* (AMA), 25:156–157 (Sept. 1), 1972.

[18] Ibid., p. 157.

[19] *United States v. Bartee* (1973), quoted in *The Citation* (AMA), 27:135–136 (Aug. 15), 1973.

[20] Ibid.

[21] *See* Erich Goode, *Drugs in American Society* (New York: Knopf, 1972), p. 191.

[22] "Drug legislation," *Massachusetts Physician,* 31:33 (May) 1972.

[23] Matthew 26:52.

Chapter Twelve

Drug Prohibition

Americans regard freedom of speech and religion as fundamental rights. Until 1914, they also regarded freedom of choosing their diets and drugs as fundamental rights. Today, however, virtually all Americans regard ingesting certain substances—prohibited by the government—as both crimes and diseases.

What is behind this fateful moral and political transformation, which has resulted in the rejection by the overwhelming majority of Americans of their right to self-control over their diets and drugs in favor of the alleged protection of their health from their own actions by a medically corrupt and corrupted state? How could it have come about in view of the obvious parallels between the freedom to put things into one's mind and its restriction by the state by means of censorship of the press, and the freedom to put things into one's body and its restriction by the state by means of drug controls?

Censorship

The answer to these questions lies basically in the fact that our society is *therapeutic* in much the same sense in which medieval Spanish society was *theocratic*. Just as the men and women living in a theocratic society did not believe in the separation of church and state but, on the contrary, fervently embraced their union, so we, living in a therapeutic society, do not believe in the separation of medicine and the state but fervently embrace their union. The censorship of drugs follows from the latter ideology as inexorably as the censorship of books followed from the former. That explains why liberals and conservatives—and people in that imaginary center as well—all favor drug controls. In fact, persons of all political and religious convictions,

Reprinted, with permission, from the January 1978 issue of *Reason* magazine. Copyright 1978 by the Reason Foundation, 3415 S. Sepulveda Blvd., Suite 400, Los Angeles, CA 90034.

save libertarians, now favor drug controls.

Liberals tend to be permissive towards socially disreputable psychoactive drugs, especially when they are used by young and hairy persons; so they generally favor decriminalizing marijuana and treating rather than punishing those engaged in the trade of LSD. They are not at all permissive, however, toward non-psychoactive drugs that are allegedly unsafe or worthless and thus favor banning saccharin and Laetrile. In these ways they betray their fantasy of the state—as good parent: such a state should restrain erring citizens by mild, minimal, and medical sanctions, and it should protect ignorant citizens by pharmacological censorship.

Conservatives, on the other hand, tend to be prohibitive toward socially disreputable psychoactive drugs, especially when they are used by young and hairy persons; so they generally favor criminalizing the use of marijuana and punishing rather than treating those engaged in the trade of LSD. At the same time, they are permissive toward non-psychoactive drugs that are allegedly unsafe or worthless and thus favor free trade in saccharin and Laetrile. In these ways, they too betray their fantasy of the state—as the enforcer of the dominant ethic: such a state should punish citizens who deviate from the moral precepts of the majority and should abstain from meddling with people's self-care.

Viewed as a political issue, drugs, books, and religious practices all present the same problem to a people and its rulers. The state, as the representative of a particular class or dominant ethic, may choose to embrace some drugs, some books, and some religious practices and reject the others as dangerous, depraved, demented, or devilish. Throughout history, such an arrangement has characterized most societies. Or the state, as the representative of a constitution ceremo-nializing the supremacy of individual choice over collective comfort, may ensure a free trade in drugs, books, and religious practices. Such an arrangement has traditionally characterized the United States. Its Constitution explicitly guarantees the right to freedom of religion and the press and implicitly guarantees the right to freedom of self-deter-mination with respect to what we put into our bodies.

Why did the framers of the Constitution not explicitly guarantee the right to take drugs? For two obvious reasons. First, because two hundred years ago medical science was not even in its infancy; medical practice was socially unorganized and therapeutically worthless.

Second, because there was then no conceivable danger of an alliance between medicine and the state. The very idea that the government should lend its police power to physicians to deprive people of their free choice to ingest certain substances would have seemed absurd to the drafters of the Bill of Rights.

This conjecture is strongly supported by a casual remark by Thomas Jefferson, clearly indicating that he regarded our freedom to put into our bodies whatever we want as essentially similar to our freedom to put into our own minds whatever we want. "Was the government to prescribe to us our medicine and diet," wrote Jefferson in 1782, "our bodies would be in such keeping as our souls are now. Thus in France the emetic was once forbidden as a medicine, the potato as an article of food."

A Therapeutic State

Jefferson poked fun at the French for their pioneering efforts to prohibit drugs and diets. What, then, would he think of the state that now forbids the use of harmless sweeteners while encouraging the use of dangerous contraceptives? that labels marijuana a narcotic and prohibits it while calling tobacco an agricultural product and promoting it? and that defines the voluntary use of heroin as a disease and the legally coerced use of methadone as a treatment for it?

Freedom of religion is indeed a political idea of transcendent importance. As that idea has been understood in the United States, it does not mean that members of the traditional churches—that is, Christians, Jews, and Muslims—may practice their faith unmolested by the government but that others—for example, Jehovah's Witnesses— may not. American religious freedom is unconditional; it is not contingent on any particular church proving, to the satisfaction of the state, that its principles or practices possess "religious efficacy."

The requirement that the supporters of a religion establish its theological credentials in order to be tolerated is the hallmark of a theological state. In Spain, under the Inquisition, there was, in an ironic sense, religious tolerance: religion was tolerated, indeed, actively encouraged. The point is that religions other than Roman Catholicism were considered to be heresies. The same considerations now apply to drugs.

The fact that we accept the requirement that the supporters of a drug establish its therapeutic credentials before we tolerate its sale or use shows that we live in a therapeutic state. In the United States today, there is, in an ironic sense, pharmacological tolerance: approved drugs are tolerated, indeed, actively encouraged. But drugs other than those officially sanctioned as therapeutic are considered worthless or dangerous. Therein, precisely, lies the moral and political point: governments are notoriously tolerant about permitting the dissemination of ideas or drugs of which they approve. Their mettle is tested by their attitude toward the dissemination of ideas and drugs of which they disapprove.

The argument that people need the protection of the state from dangerous drugs but not from dangerous ideas is unpersuasive. No one has to ingest any drug he does not want, just as no one has to read a book he does not want. Insofar as the state assumes control over such matters, it can only be in order to subjugate its citizens—by protecting them from temptation, as befits children; and by preventing them from assuming self-determination over their lives, as befits an enslaved population.

Controlling Danger

Conventional wisdom now approves—indeed, assumes as obvious—that it is the legitimate business of the state to control certain substances we take into our bodies, especially so-called psychoactive drugs. According to this view, as the state must, for the benefit of society, control dangerous persons, so it must also control dangerous drugs. The obvious fallacy in this analogy is obscured by the riveting together of the notions of dangerous drugs and dangerous acts: as a result, people now "know" that dangerous drugs cause people to behave dangerously and that it is just as much the duty of the state to protect its citizens from dope as it is to protect them from murder and theft. The trouble is that all these supposed facts are false.

It is impossible to come to grips with the problem of drug controls unless we distinguish between things and persons. A drug, whether it be heroin or insulin, is a thing. It does not do anything to anyone unless a person ingests it or injects it into himself or administers it to another. Obviously, a drug has no biological effect on a person unless it gets into his body. The basic question—that is logically prior to whether the drug is good or bad—is, therefore: How does a drug get into the person's body? Although there are many ways for that to happen, we need to consider here only a few typical instances of it.

A person may take an accepted non-prescription drug like aspirin by way of self-medication. Or, he may be given an accepted prescription drug like penicillin by way of medication by his physician. Neither of these situations disturbs most people nowadays. What disturbs the compact majority is a person taking a drug like LSD or selling a drug like heroin to others.

The most cursory attention to how drugs get into the human body thus reveals that the moral and political crux of the problem of drug controls lies not in the pharmacological properties of the chemicals in question, but in the characterological properties of the persons who take them (and of the people who permit, prescribe, and prohibit drugs).

The true believer in conventional wisdom might wish to insist at this point—not without justification—that some drugs are more dangerous than others; that, in other words, the properties of drugs are no less relevant to understanding our present-day drug problems than are the properties of the persons. That is true. But it is important that we not let that truth divert our attention from the distinction between pharmacological facts and the social policies they supposedly justify.

Prohibition

Today, ordinary, "normal" people do not really want to keep an open mind about drugs and drug controls. Instead of thinking about the problem, they tend to dismiss it with some cliché such as: "Don't tell me that heroin or LSD aren't dangerous drugs?" Ergo, they imply and indeed assert: "Don't tell me that it doesn't make good sense to prohibit their production, sale, and possession!"

What is wrong with this argument? Quite simply, everything. In the first place, the proposition that heroin or LSD is dangerous must be qualified and placed in relation to the dangerousness of other drugs and other artifacts that are not drugs. Second, the social policy that heroin or LSD should be prohibited does not follow, as a matter of logic, from the proposition that they are dangerous, even if they are dangerous.

Admittedly, heroin is more dangerous than aspirin, in the sense that it gives more pleasure to its user than aspirin; heroin is therefore more likely than aspirin to be taken for the self-induction of euphoria.

Heroin is also more dangerous than aspirin in the sense that it is easier to kill oneself with it; heroin is therefore more likely to be used for committing suicide.

The fact that people take heroin to make themselves feel happy or high—and use other psychoactive drugs for their mind-altering effects—raises a simple but basic issue that the drug-prohibitionists like to avoid, namely: What is wrong with people using drugs for that purpose? Why shouldn't people make themselves happy by means of self-medication? Let me say at once that I believe these are questions to which honest and reasonable men may offer different answers. Whatever the answers, however, I insist that they flow from moral rather than medical considerations.

For example, some people say that individuals should not take heroin because it diverts them from doing productive work, making those who use the drugs, as well as those economically dependent on them, burdens on society. Others say that whether individuals use, abuse, or avoid heroin is, unless they harm others, their private business. And still others opt for a compromise between the total prohibition of heroin and a free trade in it.

There is, however, more to the prohibitionist's position than his concern that hedonic drugs seduce people from hard labor to happy leisure. If prohibitionists were truly motivated by such concerns, they would advocate permission to use heroin contingent on the individual's proven ability to support himself (and perhaps others), rather than its unqualified suppression. The fact that they advocate no such thing highlights the symbolic aspects of drugs and drug controls.

Drugs, Fun, and Sin

The objects we now call "dangerous drugs" are metaphors for all that we consider sinful and wicked; that is why they are prohibited, rather than because they are demonstrably more harmful than countless other objects in the environment that do not now symbolize sin for us. In this connection, it is instructive to consider the cultural metamorphosis we have undergone during the past half-century, shifting our symbols of sin from sexuality to chemistry.

Our present views on drugs, especially psychoactive drugs, are strikingly similar to our former views on sex, especially masturbation. Intercourse in marriage with the aim of procreation used to be the paradigm of the proper use of one's sexual organs; whereas intercourse outside of marriage with the aim of carnal pleasure used to be the paradigm of their improper use. Until recently, masturbation—or self-abuse, as it was called—was professionally declared, and popularly accepted, as both the cause and the symptom of a variety of illnesses, especially insanity. To be sure, it is now virtually impossible to cite a contemporary medical authority to support this concept of self-abuse. Expert medical opinion now holds that there is simply no such thing: that whether a person masturbates or not is medically irrelevant and that engaging in the practice or refraining from it is a matter of personal morals or life style.

On the other hand, it is now impossible to cite a contemporary medical authority to oppose the concept of drug abuse. Expert medical opinion now holds that drug abuse is a major medical, psychiatric, and public health problem: that drug addiction is a disease similar to diabetes, requiring prolonged (or lifelong) and medically carefully supervised treatment; and that taking or not taking drugs is primarily, if not solely, a matter of medical concern and responsibility.

Like any social policy, our drug laws may be examined from two entirely different points of view: technical and moral. Our present inclination is either to ignore the moral perspective or to mistake the technical for the moral.

A Medical Problem?

An example of our misplaced overreliance on a technical approach to the so-called drug problem is the professionalized mendacity about the dangerousness of certain types of drugs. Since most propagandists against drug abuse seek to justify certain repressive policies by appeals to the alleged dangerousness of various drugs, they often falsify the facts about the true pharmacological properties of the drugs they seek to prohibit. They do so for two reasons: first, because many substances in daily use are just as harmful as the substances they want to prohibit; second, because they realize that dangerousness alone is never a sufficiently persuasive argument to justify the prohibition of any drug, substance, or artifact. Accordingly, the more they ignore the moral dimensions of the problem, the more they must escalate their fraudulent claims about the dangers of drugs.

To be sure, some drugs are more dangerous than others. It is easier to kill oneself with heroin than with aspirin. But it is also easier to kill oneself by jumping off a high building than a low one. In the case of drugs, we regard their potentiality for self-injury as a justification for their prohibition; in the case of buildings, we do not. Furthermore, we systematically blur and confuse the two quite different ways in which narcotics can cause death: by a deliberate act of suicide and by accidental overdose.

I maintain that suicide is an act, not a disease. It is therefore a moral, not a medical, problem. The fact that suicide results in death does not make it a medical problem any more than the fact that execution in the electric chair results in death makes the death penalty a medical problem. Hence, it is morally absurd—and, in a free society, politically illegitimate—to deprive an adult of a drug because he might use it to kill himself. To do so is to treat people as institutional psychiatrists treat so-called psychotics: they not only imprison such persons but take everything away from them—shoelaces, belts, razor blades, eating utensils, and so forth—until the "patients" lie naked on a mattress in a padded cell, lest they kill themselves. The result is one of the most degrading tyrannizations in the annals of human history.

Death by accidental overdose is an altogether different matter. But can anyone doubt that this danger now looms so large precisely because the sale of narcotics and many other drugs is illegal? Persons buying illicit drugs cannot be sure what they are getting or how much of it. Free trade in drugs, with governmental action limited to safeguarding the purity of the product and the veracity of labeling, would reduce the risk of accidental overdose with so-called dangerous drugs to the same levels that prevail, and that we find acceptable, with respect to other chemical agents and physical artifacts that abound in our complex technological society.

In my view, regardless of their dangerousness, all drugs should be "legalized" (a misleading term that I employ reluctantly as a concession to common usage). Although I realize that some drugs—notably, heroin, amphetamine, and LSD among those now in vogue—may have dangerous consequences, I favor free trade in drugs for the same reason the Founding Fathers favored free trade in ideas: in a free society it is none of the government's business what ideas a man puts into his mind; likewise, it should be none of its business what drug he puts into his body.

"Heresy"

Clearly, the argument that marijuana—or heroin, methadone, or morphine—is prohibited because it is addictive or dangerous cannot be supported by facts. For one thing, there are many drugs, from insulin to penicillin, that are neither addictive nor dangerous but are nevertheless also prohibited: they can be obtained only through a physician's prescription. For another, there are many things, from poisons to guns, that are much more dangerous than narcotics (especially to others) but are not prohibited. As everyone knows, it is still possible in the United States to walk into a store and walk out with a shotgun. We enjoy that right, not because we do not believe that guns are dangerous, but because we believe even more strongly that civil liberties are precious. At the same time, it is not possible in the United States to walk into a store and walk out with a bottle of barbiturates or codeine or, indeed, [in some states] even with an empty hypodermic syringe. We are now deprived of that right because we have come to value medical paternalism more highly than the right to obtain and use drugs without recourse to medical intermediaries.

I submit, therefore, that our so-called drug-abuse problem is an integral part of our present social ethic that accepts "protections" and repressions justified by appeals to health similar to those which medieval societies accepted when they were justified by appeals to faith. Drug abuse (as we now know it) is one of the inevitable consequences of the medical monopoly over drugs—a monopoly whose value is daily acclaimed by science and law, state and church, the professions and the laity. As formerly the church regulated man's relations to God, so medicine now regulates his relations to his body. Deviation from the rules set forth by the church was then considered heresy and was punished by appropriate theological sanctions, called penance; deviation from the rules set forth by medicine is now considered drug abuse (or some sort of "mental illness") and is punished by appropriate medical sanctions, called treatment.

The problem of drug abuse will thus be with us so long as we live under medical tutelage. That is not to say that, if all access to drugs were free, some people would not medicate themselves in ways that might upset us or harm them. That, of course, is precisely what happened when religious practices became free. People proceeded to engage in all sorts of religious behaviors that true believers in traditional faiths found obnoxious and upsetting. Nevertheless, in the conflict between freedom and religion, the American political system has come down squarely for the former and against the latter.

If the grown son of a devoutly religious Jewish father has a ham sandwich for lunch, the father cannot use the police power of American society to impose his moral views on his son. But if the grown son of a devoutly alcoholic father has heroin for lunch, the father can, indeed, use the police power of American society to impose his moral views on his son. Moreover, the penalty that that father could legally visit on his son might exceed the penalty that would be imposed on the son for killing his mother. It is that moral calculus—refracted through our present differential treatment of those who literally abuse others by killing, maiming, and robbing them as against those who metaphorically abuse themselves by using illicit chemicals—which reveals the depravity into which our preoccupation with drugs and drug controls has led us.

Self-Medication

I believe that just as we regard freedom of speech and religion as fundamental rights, so we should also regard freedom of self-medication as a fundamental right; and that, instead of mendaciously opposing or mindlessly promoting illicit drugs, we should, paraphrasing Voltaire, make this maxim our rule: "I disapprove of what you take, but I will defend to the death your right to take it!"

Sooner or later we shall have to confront the basic moral dilemma underlying the so-called drug problem: Does a person have the right to take a drug, any drug—not because he needs it to cure an illness, but because he wants to take it?

The Constitution and the Bill of Rights are silent on the subject of drugs. That would seem to imply that the adult citizen has, or ought to have, the right to medicate his own body as he sees fit. Were that not the case, why should there have been a need for a constitutional amendment to outlaw drinking? But if ingesting alcohol was, and is now again, a constitutional right, is ingesting opium or heroin or barbiturates or anything else not also such a right?

It is a fact that we Americans have a right to read a book—any book—not because we are stupid and want to learn from it, nor because a government-supported educational authority claims that it will be good for us, but simply because we want to read it; because the government—as our servant rather than our master—hasn't the right to meddle in our private reading affairs.

I believe that we also have a right to eat, drink, or inject a substance—any substance—not because we are sick and want it to cure us, nor because a government-supported medical authority claims that it will be good for us, but simply because we want to take it; because the government—as our servant rather than our master—hasn't the right to meddle in our private dietary and drug affairs.

It is also a fact, however, that Americans now go to jail for picking harmless marijuana growing wild in the fields, but not for picking poisonous mushrooms growing wild in the forests. Why? Because we Americans have collectively chosen to cast away our freedom to determine what we should eat, drink, or smoke. In this large and ever-expanding area of our lives, we have rejected the principle that the state is our servant rather than our master. This proposition is painfully obvious when people plaintively insist that we need the government to protect us from the hazards of "dangerous" drugs. To be sure, we need private voluntary associations—or also, some might argue, the government—to *warn* us of the dangers of heroin, high-tension wires, and high-fat diets.

But it is one thing for our would-be protectors to *inform* us of what they regard as dangerous objects in our environment. It is quite another thing for them to *punish* us if we disagree with them.

Chapter Thirteen

Bad Habits Are Not Diseases

M orris E. Chafetz, M.D., director of the National Institute of Alcohol Abuse and Alcoholism, has announced the promulgation of a "Bill of Rights for Alcoholic People," drafted for them by the Commissioners on Uniform State Laws at their annual meeting in August 1971. This bill, Dr. Chafetz explains, removes "the crime of public intoxication and the illness of alcoholism from the criminal codes and places them in the public health area where they rightfully belong." Since some people who drink do not consider themselves alcoholics and hence decline medical care, Dr. Chafetz adds that the Uniform Alcoholism and Intoxication Treatment Act adopted by the Commission "guarantees, in those few instances where civil commitment is necessary, a right to treatment 'which is likely to be beneficial.'"[1] A subsequent editorial warmly endorsed the creation of the Institute headed by Dr. Chafetz and concluded with this ringing exhortation:

> It is hoped that through government incentives, the support of medical students throughout the country, and the efforts of local medical societies together with the American Medical Association and other professional organizations, the medical schools will become much more aware of the need to equip tomorrow's physicians with the ability and imagination to cope with two of the most pressing problems of medical care facing the nation—alcoholism and drug dependence.[2]

I submit that the foregoing views consist of an approximately equal mixture of mendacity and nonsense. As a teacher in a medical school, I believe it is my duty to teach facts and theories as I see them

Reprinted with permission from *The Lancet*, July 8, 1972. All rights reserved.

and not as the state, the American Medical Association, Alcoholics Anonymous, the Women's Christian Temperance Union, the liquor industry, or any other group of special interests see them. In my judgment, the view that alcoholism is a disease is false; and the programs sponsored by the state and supported by tax monies to "cure" it are immoral and inconsistent with our political commitment to individual freedom and responsibility.[3]

It is impossible, of course, to discuss what is and is not illness, without agreement on how we shall use the word "illness." First, then, we must distinguish—as do both physicians and patients, and as our language does—between bodily and mental illness.

When a person asserts that he is ill, he usually means two things: first, that he suffers, or that he believes he suffers, from an abnormality or malfunctioning of his body; and, second, that he wants, or is at least willing to accept, medical help for it. Should the first of these conditions be absent, we would not consider the person to be physically ill; should the second be absent we would not consider him to be a medical patient. This is because the practice of modern Western medicine rests on the scientific premise that the physician's task is to diagnose and treat disorders of the human body; and on the moral premise that he can carry out these services only with the consent of his patient. Strictly speaking, then, disease or illness can affect only the body. Accordingly, there can be no such thing as mental illness. The term *mental illness* is a metaphor.

With the foregoing definition in mind, I offer the following observations about alcoholism and its relation to the medical profession.

1. Drinking to excess may cause illness, but in itself is not a disease—in the ordinary sense of the word *disease*. Excessive drinking is a habit. According to the person's values, he may consider it a good or a bad habit. If we choose to call bad habits "diseases," there is no limit to what we may define as "disease"—and "treat" involuntarily. The misuse of alcohol—whatever the reason for it—is no more an illness than is the misuse of any other product of human inventiveness, from language to nuclear energy.

2. Every individual, the alcoholic included, is capable of injuring or killing himself. This potentiality is a fundamental expression of man's freedom of action. Such conduct may be regarded as immoral or sinful or undisciplined and penalized by means of informal sanctions. But it should not, in a free society, be regarded as either a crime

or a disease, warranting the use of the police powers of the state for its control or suppression.

3. Every individual, the alcoholic included, is also capable of injuring or killing others—both while under the influence of alcohol and while not under its influence. This potentiality, too, is a fundamental expression of man's freedom. Such conduct not only justifies self-defense by those attacked, but also often requires the formalized protection of society from the harmful individual by means of criminal laws and sanctions. In other words, the alcoholic should be left free to injure himself; those who wish to help him should be left free to offer their services to him, but should not be allowed to use force or fraud in their efforts to "help"; at the same time, the alcoholic should not be left free to injure others; nor should his alcoholism be accepted as an excuse for any criminal act he may have committed.

4. It is one thing to maintain that a person is not responsible for being an alcoholic; it is quite another to maintain that he is not responsible for the interpersonal, occupational, economic, and legal consequences of his actions. The former proposition implies only an unwillingness to punish a person for excessive drinking; the latter implies either giving the alcoholic an excuse for injuring others, or justifying legislation for controlling his alcoholism rather than his illegal behavior.

5. If we regard alcoholism as a bona-fide disease—"like any other"—then we ought to let the alcoholic accept or reject treatment for it. Venereal diseases are now said to be of epidemic proportions. They are, moreover, genuine, bodily diseases for which we now possess efficacious and safe methods of treatment—yet such treatment is not compulsory. Advocating the compulsory "treatment" of alcoholics (and other "addicts") through what is euphemistically called "civil commitment," and calling such involuntary interventions a "Bill of Rights for Alcoholic People," are, in my opinion, the manifestations of a state of affairs in American medicine and government far more alarming than the "diseases" against which such "cures" and their sordid justifications are invoked.[4]

By a curious coincidence, in one of his most important short pieces, George Orwell compared the abuse of language with the abuse of alcohol. "A man may take to drink," he wrote, "because he feels himself to be a failure and then fail all the more completely because he drinks. It is rather the same thing that is happening to the English language. It becomes ugly and inaccurate because our thoughts are foolish, but the slovenliness of our language makes it easier for us to have foolish thoughts."[5]

When Dr. Chafetz asserts that alcoholism is an illness—without telling us what "alcoholism" is and what "illness" is; that "it is the task of the practicing physician to take the initiative in acting to provide adequate medical and follow-up care for alcoholic persons…,"[6] when in fact his task is to offer care only to those persons who want it; when he calls giving physicians the power to imprison alcoholics a "Bill of Rights" for the victims; and when the American Medical Association uncritically and unqualifiedly endorses such humbug—we then stand before the very phenomenon Orwell described.

But, of course, Orwell did more than describe; he warned that "…if thought corrupts language, language can also corrupt thought."[7] And he concluded that political language—and to this we may here add medical language—"is designed to make lies sound truthful and murder respectable and to give an appearance of solidity to pure wind."[8]

As an academician and a teacher, I believe our duty now is to stand up against the Lysenkoism that is sweeping the country. Whether we may want to dub it "Jaffeism," or "Chafetzism," or the "Crusade Against Alcoholism and Addiction," or by some other catchy phrase hardly matters; what matters is that as physicians and teachers we resist politically motivated and mandated redefinitions of (bad) habits as diseases; that we condemn and eschew involuntary medical and psychiatric interventions; and that, instead of joining and supporting the "holy war" on alcoholism and drug abuse, we actively repudiate this contemporary version of "popular delusion and crowd madness."[9]

In the past half-century, the medical sciences have advanced as never before in history; yet, morally, the medical profession has fallen upon bad times. Everywhere, it has allowed itself to be enslaved by the state; at the same time, it has encroached on the liberties of the patients, making them, in turn, the slaves of the doctors. But, as Montaigne, quoting Apollonius, observed: "It is for slaves to lie and for free men to speak the truth."[10] Where are the free men of medicine?

Notes

[1]M.E. Chafetz, *JAMA, 219* (1972), p. 1471.
[2]*JAMA, 219* (1972), p. 1757.
[3]T.S. Szasz, *West. Med., 7,* 1966, p. 15.
[4]T.S. Szasz, *Harper's,* April 1972, p. 74.
[5]George Orwell, "Politics and the English Language" (1946), in *The Orwell Reader* (New York, 1956), p. 355.
[6]Chafetz, op. cit.
[7]Orwell, op. cit., p. 364.
[8]Ibid., p. 366.
[9]C. Mackay, *Extraordinary Popular Delusions and the Madness of Crowds* (1841), (New York, 1962).
[10]Michel de Montaigne, *Essays* (1580), trans. by J.M. Cohen (Harmondsworth, England, 1967), p. 208.

Chapter Fourteen

A Dialogue on Drugs

*I*n constructing this imaginary dialogue between Socrates and Hippocrates, I have of course taken certain liberties with historical events. However, these two immortal Athenians were contemporaries, and the sap of the poppy was known and used by the ancient Greeks. The following facts may be of interest to the reader in this connection.

Socrates lived from about 470 B.C. till 399 B.C.; Hippocrates, from about 460 till 377 B.C. The word opium *is derived from the Greek word for juice, the drug being obtained from the juice of the poppy capsules. The term* codeine *comes from the Greek word for poppy head. Although opium was used before recorded history, the first undisputed reference to poppy juice is in the writings of Theophrastus (371–287 B.C.).*

HIPPOCRATES: My dear Socrates, I am so relieved I found you here. I must seek your advice about the terrible plague that has struck our beloved Athens.

SOCRATES: Come, sit by me and rest. You are like all physicians: you work too hard and you do not take proper care of yourself. You say you need my advice about a plague. But what do I know about diseases and treatments?

HIPPOCRATES: This plague is unlike most others, dear friend. Despite our efforts—and you know how wondrously skillful our Athenian physicians have become—we can do nothing to halt it.

SOCRATES: Tell me more about it. I fear I must be getting old and out of touch with things, for though I have been mingling and talking with my fellow citizens, as has been my custom for longer than I care to think, I have not seen any sign of a plague. Indeed, our people

A complete version of this chapter was published in *Psychiatric Opinion, 14* (March/April 1977). It is also in *The Therapeutic State: Psychiatry in the Mirror of Current Events* (Buffalo, NY: Prometheus Books, 1984).

seem to me to be more robust than ever.

HIPPOCRATES: I feel more rested now. And I see I assumed you knew more about our medical problems than you do. No matter. I can explain my mission easily enough. And I say "mission" advisedly: for, much as I love to converse with you, dear Socrates, I come not just of my own accord, but at the request of our Senate. Some of our senators believe that the very survival of Athens is at stake. And, I must say, I quite agree with them.

SOCRATES: Dear friend, you keep on exciting yourself. You tell me how very serious the problem is that you want to talk about, but you do not tell me what that problem is. Is it possible that part of your difficulty lies in this exaggerated importance you attach to it?

HIPPOCRATES: Please, Socrates, save your skepticism until you have heard me out.

SOCRATES: Forgive me. I will try.

HIPPOCRATES: First, then, let me tell you something about the dire effects of this plague. It disables many of our young men, men in the prime of their physical and mental powers. Instead of working, defending their city, taking care of their wives and children, they loaf and sponge off others.

SOCRATES: You must explain this to me more fully, Hippocrates. You know I am not familiar with the details of your craft. But are you not describing men who are lazy rather than sick?

HIPPOCRATES: They only seem lazy. They are ill, I can assure you, dear Socrates. Perhaps I should tell you about how this plague kills; then you will understand what a serious disease we have to contend with. It amazes me, in fact, that you seem so unaware that, among our young adults, this plague has become a leading cause of death. Don't you read the newspapers? Don't you know that not a day passes in Athens without such a death?

SOCRATES: I am getting more and more confused. Of course I read the newspapers. But, as you know, I don't believe anything they print. Besides, they don't know how to use the Greek language our gods gave us. You keep talking about a terrible plague, but you don't tell me just what it is. Instead, you now tell me that it kills a lot of young people. But people die of all sorts of things. For example, they get killed in war. Now, you don't mean to tell me that war is a plague? What, my dear Hippocrates, do you call this plague, this disease?

HIPPOCRATES: We call it "drug addiction," of course.

SOCRATES: Do you physicians know how a person acquires this illness?

HIPPOCRATES: Yes. By contagion: one person catches it from another.

SOCRATES: And how do you physicians know that a person has caught it?

HIPPOCRATES: That is a good question, my dear Socrates. I am glad our Senate finally decided to solicit your views on this problem; though, I must say, our senators are so frantic, I think they no longer know how to listen to anyone but themselves. But I should answer your question. The fact is, we physicians often don't know whether a person has this disease. The patients often prefer not to come to us. I am ashamed to confess, we usually discover the disease only after our policemen take the patients into custody and bring them to us.

SOCRATES: You mean to tell me that if our law enforcers would not make these arrests, you would not know that these citizens were ill? Don't they complain of feeling ill? Don't they want your help?

HIPPOCRATES: It's not so simple, Socrates. Does a wounded warrior lying unconscious on the battlefield complain of being ill? Does he ask for our help? Of course not. But you will have to admit he is nevertheless sick and will be grateful to us for binding his wounds. It's just the same with the drug addict.

SOCRATES: Perhaps so.

HIPPOCRATES: Let me tell you more about the nature of this disease, about how it affects the person, his body and his mind, and what we are trying to do to cure it. In the first place, the person who develops this affliction acquires an irresistible urge to take certain drugs, which, in small doses, make him feel especially well, but in larger doses may kill him. Extracts made from the sap of the poppy are very popular, as you know.

SOCRATES: Yes, I know that. But no one has to use the poppy in this way.

HIPPOCRATES: But that is just the point. The addict has an irresistible craving for it, a craving like the feverish man has for water.

SOCRATES: So let him eat poppy.

HIPPOCRATES: But it's illegal to do so. It's illegal even to have it, much less to use it.

SOCRATES: Dear Hippocrates, either you are confused, or you are trying to confuse me. First, you compare the addict's need for the extract of poppy—I think you doctors call it opium—to the feverish man's need for water, and then you tell me that it is illegal to possess and use opium. What, then, is the problem: the craving or the difficulty to satisfy it?

HIPPOCRATES: You are right, of course. But opium is unlike water. It can kill you if you take too much of it.

SOCRATES: But why should you worry about that? Surely you know that killing oneself is not against our morals or laws?

HIPPOCRATES: Dear Socrates, you are not letting me put the problem before you—the problem as the Senate sees it and as our physicians see it.

SOCRATES: All right, please state it, and I will keep quiet.

HIPPOCRATES: The problem with drug addiction is that large numbers of young people, and even children, take illegal drugs— opium is just one of the substances they use—and, as a result, do not study in school, neglect their civic duties, and infect others with their drug habit. And this is just a small part of the problem. These patients also become economically dependent on others—on their families, on the state. And, last but not least, many of them rob and steal to get the money to buy the drugs they want. Do you see now what the problem is, and that it is like a veritable plague?

SOCRATES: Wait, dear friend. Are you asking me if this *is* a plague, or if it is *like* a plague?

HIPPOCRATES: What is the difference?

SOCRATES: It is the difference between a thing and something else that resembles it. Like the difference between water and opium, in your own example.

HIPPOCRATES: But what difference does it make, as a practical matter? We want people to stop taking opium. Don't you?

SOCRATES: Why should I? That's their affair. But you are getting excited again, dear Hippocrates. Let us go back to the beginning. Why did you come to talk to me: to get my help to make our fellow Athenians to do this or that thing, or to discuss the plague which you say has afflicted our city?

HIPPOCRATES: The latter, of course.

SOCRATES: Good. Because you know that's all I am competent to do, if indeed I am competent to do that.

HIPPOCRATES: You have listened patiently to my complaints, dear Socrates. Perhaps you should ask me some questions now. I know that is how you reason things out.

SOCRATES: Yes. Let us proceed. And I know I can be direct with you, because you are both honest and courageous. You say that the addicts—the patients who, you say, are addicted to various things—take drugs. If they didn't take them, they would not be ill. Is that correct?

HIPPOCRATES: Yes, of course.

SOCRATES: What, then, makes them ill? Why do you say they suffer from a disease?

HIPPOCRATES: Isn't it obvious? Suppose your enemies poison your food or drink—with hemlock, or with any of the numerous poisons we have—and you fall sick. Will you not be suffering from an illness? And if you die, will you not have died of the poisoning?

SOCRATES: Yes, of course. But young people who use drugs want to please themselves, not to poison themselves. Is that not so?

HIPPOCRATES: Yes, that is so. When taken in proper amounts, the poppy—and many other drugs our noble physicians have developed—do indeed have a pleasant effect. Don't you see, Socrates, that is precisely what makes our problem so difficult: our patients feel well so long as they take the drugs to which they have become accustomed.

SOCRATES: It seems, then, that these drugs satisfy some sort of appetite—much as food satisfies hunger and a handsome maiden, or boy as the case may be, satisfies lust.

HIPPOCRATES: Those are apt comparisons, dear Socrates.

SOCRATES: But bear with me, then, Hippocrates. For if the effect of the poppy is of this kind, why trouble yourself about it? What our people eat or with whom they bed is no concern of yours or of other doctors. Why, then, concern yourself with whether they take poppy?

HIPPOCRATES: Because if they take too much, they die.

SOCRATES: If they eat too much, they die, too.

HIPPOCRATES: That's sophistry, dear Socrates, and you know it.

SOCRATES: Perhaps you are right. But if you want to reason along with me about whether or not the use of the poppy constitutes an illness and is something that you physicians ought to worry about, then you must not simply base your claim on the fact that its misuse may be fatal. You must think more clearly than that. You know perfectly well that the misuse of countless things may prove to be fatal. If you swim out too far into the sea, you may drown. Will that make you conclude that swimming is an illness?

HIPPOCRATES: But our Senate has seen fit to prohibit the use of the poppy. It has decreed that those who use it are addicts and must be treated.

SOCRATES: So next they'll prohibit swimming in the sea.

HIPPOCRATES: Don't jest, Socrates. This is a serious matter.

SOCRATES: I know it is serious. But it is also silly. You are a wise and compassionate physician, Hippocrates, beloved in all of Athens. And you let our senators, about whose wisdom the less said the better, tell you that young people in the best of health are sick, just because they put something into their bodies the senators don't think they should?

HIPPOCRATES: Sometimes you use words, Socrates, as we physicians use the poppy: you, to soften the pain of truth; we, to soften the pain of illness and old age.

SOCRATES: Thank you, my friend. And our people who use the poppy without being ill, without the permission of you doctors, use it perhaps to soften the pain of boredom, of futility, of life itself.

HIPPOCRATES: Of course, that is so. We have always known that.

SOCRATES: It is clear now, dear Hippocrates, that you have two quite separate problems. One is the effects of the poppy on those who use them, and what, if anything, physicians ought to do about it. The other is the effect of its prohibition, and what, if anything, physicians ought to do about it. By combining these two problems, you only make each the more difficult to solve.

HIPPOCRATES: So it is. Will you please tell me, Socrates, your views on each?

SOCRATES: How to resolve such dilemmas is your responsibility and the responsibility of your colleagues and patients. For it is you, much more than I, who are affected thereby. I neither use nor prescribe drugs. Were I to use the poppy myself, it would only becloud my powers of reasoning; and were I to recommend its use, I would be guilty of beclouding the powers of reasoning of others.

HIPPOCRATES: I understand that. It is just this detachment which makes your judgment so valuable. So please do answer my question. I understand that I am solely responsible for how I use your words. As you seem to believe that those who want to use the poppy should be allowed to do so, will you grant me the same privilege with your words?

SOCRATES: Well argued, dear Hippocrates! All right, then. Here is my answer to your first question—that is, about the effects of the poppy and the physicians' moral duty in this matter. Physicians ought to study the effects of the poppy and explain their findings to the people. If they misuse it and, as a result, fall ill, physicians ought to treat them, if they desire such treatment. But I really should not tell you all this, dear friend. You are justly sought after because you insist on putting the interests of your patients above all other considerations. In short, if a person misuses the poppy, or any other drug, with the result of what we might call "self-poisoning," and if he seeks medical help, then it is right and proper that you and your colleagues should help him. Otherwise, you should leave him alone. And you should certainly leave alone those who use the poppy in moderation. They are neither sick, nor are they your patients or the patients of any other physician.

HIPPOCRATES: I am afraid to hear your answer to the second question, Socrates, for I can surmise it now. But I would like to hear it in your own words.

SOCRATES: All right. That is the question about the effects of the prohibition of the poppy and what the physician ought to do about this problem. Do you remember the time when our senators prohibited the use of wine? That was before your time and mine. But you have read Herodotus. You have talked to people who lived then. It's the same now. Except it's worse. Much worse. Why? Because no Athenian took seriously the idea that drunkenness was an illness that you physicians ought to cure.

HIPPOCRATES: How true! Our people were wise enough to see through that ruse. The cure for gluttony and drunkenness is self-discipline, not medicines.

SOCRATES: But our people have forgotten all this. And so have our senators and physicians. They now all believe that just because something is called "drug abuse" and "drug addiction" that makes them diseases. And to justify legislating about them, they call them "contagious diseases."

HIPPOCRATES: I see your point. After all, illness is something that usually happens to a person. Addiction is something a person does to himself.

SOCRATES: Exactly. Instead of comparing drug use to illness, I would suggest a quite different analogy. When a person is given drugs without his knowledge or against his will, and the drugs injure or kill him, that is like attempted murder or successful murder. Whereas, when a person takes drugs, and the drugs injure or kill him, that is like attempted suicide or successful suicide.

HIPPOCRATES: It would follow, then, that our Senate would rightly condemn the one, but not the other. And that it should prohibit "giving" poison, but not "taking" it.

SOCRATES: That would be consistent with our moral beliefs, as Athenians. But you see, these are problems for the philosopher and for the statesman, not for the physician.

HIPPOCRATES: Do not be so easy on us doctors, Socrates. It seems to me we have let ourselves be fooled into believing that some things are diseases that are not, perhaps because it flattered our vanity—and our pocketbooks—to be called upon to "save" our people from all kinds of predicaments. But what do I tell the Senate?

SOCRATES: I am afraid you have to decide that. But do not worry about it. Senators have power and are therefore not curious. They'll hear only what they want to hear.

HIPPOCRATES: I cannot afford to be so skeptical. Anyway, I am grateful for your counsel. I will tell them there is no plague. I will tell them that our problem is that some men are immoderate in their use of drugs and others in their use of laws; and that the immoderateness of the one stimulates the immoderateness of the other.

SOCRATES: Thank you, my friend. I hope the senators will listen. But it does not matter. Maybe one of the pages or visitors will. And the truth will be burned into his heart. That is how it survives.

Chapter Fifteen

The Protocols of the Learned Experts on Heroin

The children of each generation are taught to want what they are taught they must not have.

—R.G. Collingwood (1939)

W hy did the forgery of Janet Cooke's ugly story, "8-Year-Old Heroin Addict Lives for a Fix" go undetected at the *Washington Post?* Why did it win a Pulitzer Prize? Although these are two quite unrelated questions, the same answer fits both. I believe that this fabrication went undetected and won a Pulitzer Prize because it purported to prove, once more, that heroin is our deadliest enemy.

Religious and medical propaganda to the contrary notwithstanding, I hold some simple truths to be self-evident. One of these truths is that just as the dead do not rise from the grave, so drugs do not commit crimes. The dead remain dead. Drugs are inert chemicals that have no effect on human beings who choose not to use them. No one has to smoke cigarettes, and no one has to shoot heroin. People smoke cigarettes because they want to, and they shoot heroin because they want to. Furthermore, so far as the connection between heroin and crime is concerned, I contend that, the propaganda of the anti-drug crusaders to the contrary notwithstanding, this truth is also self-evident: people under the influence of a powerful central-nervous-system depressant drug, such as heroin, are less rather than more likely to commit crimes than are people who are not under the influence of such a drug; on the other hand, people who live in a society in which

This chapter was published in the July 1981 edition of *The Libertarian Review*. It is also in *The Therapeutic State: Psychiatry in the Mirror of Current Events* (Buffalo, NY: Prometheus Books, 1984).

the use of certain drugs is popular, in which the sale of those drugs is prohibited, and in which the drug prohibitions are not enforced, are indeed more likely to commit crimes than they would be in the absence of those conditions. However, since no one is so blind as the man who does not want to see, these truths are quite powerless against popular mythologies, as the *New York Times* editorial comment on the Cooke affair illustrates. Under the title "The Pulitzer Lie" (April 17, 1981), the editors of the *Times* emphasize their puzzlement:

> We do not know what possessed Janet Cooke to invent an interview with an imaginary 8-year-old drug addict who aspired to grow up to be a heroin pusher in the nation's capital. Nor do we know why the *Washington Post* was so quick to claim the protection of the First Amendment when city authorities sought help in locating children so obviously needing help. We do not know why this contested tale was then pushed for journalism's highest honor, or why the Pulitzer Prize judges jumped the entry from one category to another to bestow the award.

Although I do not want to sound arrogant, I believe that I know the answer to these questions. Indeed, I believe that the editors of the *Times* know it too, albeit they do not want to admit it, or, as Freud has put it, they repress it. And the repressed, as Freud observed, invariably returns.

In this case, the repressed appears in another editorial only a few inches above "The Pulitzer Lie." In that comment, entitled "To Fight Crime, Fight Drugs," the editors admonish the Reagan administration for its insufficient zeal in fighting the drug menace. "The East Coast is currently swamped with heroin," we are informed. "In New York, drug-related robberies and burglaries have more than doubled in three years." But I am afraid that just as Janet Cooke's story about "Jimmy" was not true, so the *New York Times* editorial about "drug-related crimes" is also not true. The crimes in question are not "drug-related" but "drug-prohibition-related," which is not the same thing.

It is sad how quickly people have forgotten that when Nelson Rockefeller ran for governor, his principal campaign strategy consisted in placing full-page advertisements in the newspapers showing the arm of a young black male injecting heroin. In the accompanying caption

Rockefeller pledged to free the people of New York state from this "plague" and the crime it "causes."

People seem also to have forgotten that only a few months ago Governor Hugh Carey offered this "truth" to explain why so many thugs stole so many gold chains in New York City. "The epidemic of gold-chain snatching in the city," declared Carey, "is the result of a Russian design to wreck America by flooding the nation with deadly heroin." If the Russians "were using nerve gas on us," the Governor continued, "we'd certainly call out the troops. This is more insidious than nerve gas. Nerve gas passes off. This doesn't. It kills. I'm not overstating the case."

In love and war all is supposed to be fair. The love of saving people from the Devil and the war on Evil have indeed always been regarded as ample justifications for fabricating strategic lies. Let us face it: Cooke's story was *not* a "weird and atypical hoax," as the *Post* characterized it in hindsight. On the contrary, it was typical anti-drug propaganda, virtually indistinguishable from the standard pharmaco-mythological tales with which "professionals" and the media have been deluging the American public for the past two decades. If Cooke's story had been "weird and atypical," the editors of the *Post* would have displayed more skepticism toward it and the Pulitzer Prize judges would not have gone out of their way to honor it.

The adjective invariably used to describe the images that Cooke evoked is "shocking." Were a reporter to paint a similarly shocking picture today about, say, Jews poisoning wells or black men raping white women, no respectable newspaper would print the story, nor would it win any prizes. That Janet Cooke's concoction was published and that it won the coveted Pulitzer Prize thus signifies that she tapped a vital artery in America's body politic, a vessel nourishing our most sacred fears and prejudices. There is much evidence to support this view.

First, we have learned that, at the Pulitzer Prize board, one of the most enthusiastic defenders of Cooke's article was an editor from the *Washington Star* who, according to the *Times,* maintained that the piece deserved the prize because it "'had done a great service' by alerting Washington residents to the problems of juvenile drug addiction." Then, there is the reaction of *Post* staffers to it, both before and after its exposure as a fabrication. According to *Time* magazine, the editors at the *Post* "were comforted by letters from readers who claimed they knew Jimmy or children like him." At the *Post*, City Editor Milton Coleman was "very frankly surprised" that the police had not located "Jimmy," and was so impressed by the piece that "he wanted another story on young addicts."

After the hoax was exposed, Post Executive Editor Benjamin Bradlee revealed that the *Post* can dish it out better than it can take it. In an ironic inversion of the Watergate scenario, in a front-page interview in the *Detroit Free Press*, Bradlee incriminated himself by "obstructing" not justice (since no crime had been committed), but what may be even more important, truth (since a lie had been published). Asked "Have you talked to Cooke recently? What happens to her?" Bradlee replied:

> Well, I talked to her mother and father, but I haven't talked to her since early this morning. We're going to take care of her. We're going to see that she has professional help. We've talked to professional help about her, and we're going to get it for her and pay for it.

But Janet Cooke is neither a child nor an incompetent mental patient. Why talk to her parents? Why talk to "professional help"? Why call psychiatrists "professional help"? Why pay for the psychiatric treatment of a former *Post* employee who "resigns" to avoid being fired? I object to Bradlee's imposing an "insanity plea" on Cooke. Janet Cooke is a liar, not a lunatic, and Bradlee's casual categorization of her as a mental patient only serves to further diminish his own, and the *Post*'s, credibility.

More recently than most people care to admit, multitudes in the West celebrated their collective revulsion against what they then considered to be evil incarnate, the Jew, and its carrier, "International Zionism," through the mythopoesis of "The Protocols of the Learned Elders of Zion." Today, multitudes in the West celebrate their collective revulsion against what they now consider to be evil incarnate, heroin, and its carrier, the "pusher," through the mythopoesis of what could be called "The Protocols of the Learned Experts on Heroin." The Nazis did not have to invent new lies about Jews. Janet Cooke did not have to invent new lies about drugs.

The infamous "Protocols of the Learned Elders of Zion" was purported to be a true account of a conspiratorial plan for Jewish world conquest, drafted at a secret meeting of the first Zionist Congress in Basel, Switzerland, in 1897. The story was first published in the Russian newspaper *Znamia* ("The Banner") in 1903 and was quickly translated into German, French, English, and other Western languages. The spurious character of this document was not revealed until 1921. Subsequently, it was established that the "Protocols" were commissioned by the Russian secret police. The full story of the forgery, at least so far as it could be uncovered, was not told until 1942.

We may not know it, or may not want to know it, but we live in an age in which we are deluged with a similar sort of allegedly true, but actually spurious, propaganda—about "drugs." One such example must suffice here.

Early in January 1968, Raymond P. Shafer, then the governor of Pennsylvania and subsequently the chairman of President Nixon's Marijuana Commission, announced to the press that six college students stared at the sun while under the influence of LSD and were blinded as a result. The story was all over the country. Less than two weeks later, the *New York Times* reported that "The Governor, who yesterday told a news conference that he was convinced the report was true, said his investigators discovered this morning that the story was 'a fabrication' by Dr. Norman Yoder [Commissioner of the Office of the Blind].... He said Dr. Yoder, who was unavailable for comment, had admitted the hoax." What happened as a result of this disclosure? Nothing. Dr. Yoder and his lies were disposed of by the method characteristic of our age. Pennsylvania Attorney General William C. Sennet diagnosed Yoder as "sick" and attributed his fabrication to "his concern over illegal LSD use by children." Janet Cooke and the *Washington Post* were no doubt similarly concerned over heroin use by children.

At this point, it is necessary to focus on, and to expose, the key role that the imagery of helpless children—cared for by good people and corrupted by evil people—plays in the rhetoric of scapegoating. Gathering under this banner, the drug-mongers lost no time defending the morality of anti-heroin mendacity, even before the clamor over the non-existent "Jimmy" had died down. For example, William F. Buckley Jr. (who really should know better), pleaded that we "go easy" on Janet Cooke because "the story of an 8-year-old addicted to heroin is, in our wretched times, far from unlikely." No doubt, the idea of the menace of children as drug-abusers seems "far from un-

likely" to Buckley, just as the idea of the menace of children as self-
abusers (masturbators) must have seemed far from unlikely to his
father or grandfather. It is regrettable, however, that Buckley's bound-
less fear and loathing of heroin drive him to almost glorifying Janet
Cooke by comparing her well-intentioned deception with the de-
monic deeds of the "pusher." "As one member of the white majority," writes Buckley, "I'd prefer the company of a black newspaper-
woman who fabricated a story centered on a mythic *but entirely
plausible little victim* [emphasis added] of drugs, to the company of
the relatively untroubled black (or white) drug pushers who ride
around in their Cadillacs sowing their poison."

But what has driving Cadillacs got to do with the morality of
using heroin? Is murder more wicked if the killer leaves the scene in a
Cadillac than if he leaves it on foot? If providing people with heroin is
a grave wrong, as Mr. Buckley clearly believes it is, then giving it away
gratis is at least as wicked as is selling it for a high price. In fact,
Buckley is using cheap anticapitalist rhetoric to whip up hatred against
a scapegoat. Moreover, it is implicit in Buckley's argument that selling
heroin is very bad, but selling cigarettes is not so bad or not bad at all.
Surely, it is unimaginable that Buckley would employ his anti-Cadillac
rhetoric against the American tobacco barons and the "pushers" who
distribute their toxic products.

Buckley's foregoing remarks articulate what is now considered to
be the received truth about heroin. A lead letter in the *New York
Times* by Don Russakoff—identified as the President of the Therapeutic Communities of America—illustrates further that the American
"experts" know everything about "narcotics" that isn't so. Lamenting
that the Cooke story proved to be false, Russakoff actually praises the
Post for publishing it. "Tragically," he writes, "many other stories
about pre-teen narcotic addicts never reach the front page, although
they are indisputably true." But none of those stories is indisputably
true. And even if they were, it would not follow—except as a leap of
faith—that prohibiting the use of certain selected "dangerous drugs"
is the correct social policy for dealing with the problem.

Revealingly, Russakoff, like Buckley, also bases his argument on a
propagandistic use of the imagery of the child as drug victim. "Not
long ago," he writes, "at one of our professional conferences, a physician described the case of a 6-year-old child who had overdosed on
'angel dust.'" And what is that supposed to prove? That perhaps that

physician too was a liar? That some parents neglect their children? That we should prohibit vacations in the Alps lest children overdose on poisonous mushrooms—or fall off the cliffs? Buckley and Russakoff are not presenting evidence or offering argument; they are whipping up mindless passion in the people against a scapegoat. Cooke may have written a false story and the *Post* may have been misled into publishing it. But the Satanic threat remains and the vigilance of the vigilantes is now more justified than ever. "The *Times, Washington Post,* and many other responsible publications," concludes Russakoff, "have reported often on the worsening drug epidemic. It is real, not imaginary. And a high proportion of its victims are children. *Small children.*" (Emphasis added.)

As I suggested some time ago, the contemporary American attitude toward "dangerous drugs" is best understood in religious-mythological terms—that is, as the "ritual expulsion of evil" incarnated in a scapegoat. In the Yom Kippur ceremony, the scapegoat is a goat. In Christian anti-Semitism, it is the Jew. In contemporary America, it is heroin (and other illicit drugs). Once people accept something—an animal, a person, a people, a drug—as a scapegoat which incarnates Evil, they ipso facto consider destroying the scapegoat as Good. Consider, in this connection, the following:

• Formerly, Christians feared the Jews because they allegedly poisoned wells; accordingly, the Jews were savagely persecuted. Today, Americans fear heroin because it allegedly poisons people, especially young people; accordingly, heroin and heroin "pushers" are savagely persecuted. In fact, the Jews did not poison any wells, and heroin does not poison anyone. (The difficulty the contemporary reader has in seeing the difference between heroin poisoning someone and a person poisoning himself with heroin is a major symptom of the success of the anti-drug propaganda.)

• People who believe in a scapegoat do not want to understand it, they want to destroy it. When people regard Jews as Christ-killers or vermin, they do not want to understand Jews, they want a society free of Jews ("Judenfrei"). Similarly, when people regard heroin as a "killer drug" or as a worthless "poison," they do not want to understand heroin, they want a society free of heroin.

Perhaps deep in her soul Janet Cooke actually believed that "The Protocols of the Learned Experts on Heroin" were true, and perhaps she simply wanted to support their admonitory tale by adding to it a fresh chapter of her own. Let us not forget that, in the past, many devout persons had dramatic encounters with devils and saints, and no one called them liars; and that, in our own day, many "devout" persons have dramatic encounters with heroin pushers and cured addicts, and no one calls them liars. Janet Cooke told a rousing good tale, as a good writer should. She inflamed the public passion against the Enemy, as a good rhetorician is supposed to. To expect that her story should also be true—when hardly anyone else's about "drugs" is—seems almost unfair.

Concerning Janet Cooke's mythic hero, "Jimmy," one more reflection is in order. Some people in Washington actually believed that they knew him. Cooke herself maintained for as long as she could that "Jimmy" was real. Obviously, there was virtually no way of proving that "Jimmy" did not exist. All this made Cooke's denial or admission of the forgery exquisitely important. Which leads to my final observation—namely, that it seems quite possible that had Janet Cooke not lied about her academic credentials, her lies about heroin (for which the mythic "Jimmy" was, after all, only a vehicle) would probably have gone down America's collective gullet of gullibility just as smoothly as have all the other lies about heroin now passing as the received truth.

There is a moral to this story and it is this. No doubt unwittingly, Janet Cooke has done us a favor. She has held up a mirror in which we can catch a glimpse of a prevailing popular delusion. In the future, when people will worship at other shrines, they will scoff at our drug mythology just as we now scoff at the blood and race mythologies of our fathers and grandfathers.

Will we ever learn one of history's more obvious lessons—to be especially on guard against those who lie to us by appealing to the welfare of children? How many Jews were murdered to save Christian children from being turned into matzo? The ritual murder of people has always been preceded by the ritual murder of the truth—and, indeed, by the ritual murder of the language itself.

Chapter Sixteen

Our Property Right in Drugs

Drugs are a species of property, and hence the right to drugs is a form of property right. Accordingly, I maintain that we have a right to grow, buy, and ingest drugs much as we have a right to grow, buy, and ingest food; and that drug prohibitions, epitomized by our prescription laws, constitute deprivations of our fundamental right to own and use property.

To appreciate the significance of our loss of the right to drugs as a loss of the right to property, consider the following imaginary, but hardly implausible, scenario. Robert, a retired widower in his 60s, lives alone in a suburban home. He has many friends, enjoys good health, is economically secure and has no dependents. His hobby is gardening in the greenhouse attached to his home. A genius at making things grow, Robert's home overflows with exotic plants and fresh flowers, and his tomatoes are legendary. Let us imagine that Robert, an adventurous and enterprising person, acquires some marijuana, coca, and poppy seeds, plants them in his greenhouse, nurtures the seedlings into mature plants, harvests them, and produces some marijuana, coca leaves, and raw opium. Much given to privacy, Robert does not even let a cleaning person into his home, though he could well afford it. Hence, there is no way for anyone, legally, to know about his miniature drug farm. Finally, let us assume that, on an occasional Saturday evening, Robert, alone at home, smokes a little marijuana, or chews a few coca leaves, or mixes some opium powder into his midnight tea.

What has Robert done, and how do American law and medicine regard him and his behavior? Ownership of land and buildings is a basic property right. Privacy, especially since *Stanley v. Georgia* and

This chapter is adopted from Dr. Szasz's luncheon address presented at the Fifth International Conference on Drug Policy Reform in Washington, D.C., on Nov. 15, 1991. The ideas contained herein are more fully articulated in his book, *Our Right to Drugs: The Case for a Free Market* (New York: Praeger Press, 1992).

Roe v. Wade, is also a basic right.[1] Thus, Robert has simply exercised some of his property and privacy rights—the right to his land, his home, and the fruits of his labor. He has deprived no one else of his life, liberty, or property. Conventional wisdom and medical disinformation to the contrary notwithstanding, Robert has not harmed himself either.

Nevertheless, American criminal law now regards him as guilty of criminal possession and use of controlled and illegal substances. American psychiatry regards him as a mental patient suffering from chemical dependency, substance abuse, personality disorder, and perhaps other dreaded psychopathological aberrations. American medicine, generally, regards him as a person in dire need of mythical drug abuse treatment, whether he wants such treatment or not, especially if he doesn't want it.

Moreover, it is now considered to be perfectly legal and constitutional to stigmatize Robert as a mentally sick person, to criminalize his behavior as that of an evil-minded lawbreaker, to dispossess him of his home and impose an astronomical fine on him, to incarcerate him as a dangerous offender, and to impose pseudo-medical interventions called "treatments" on him against his will.

Steadily Surrendering Our Rights

From the founding of the American Colonies until 1914, the trade in drugs in this country was as free as the trade in commodities and consumer goods generally. Indeed, from colonial times until the Civil War, marijuana was an important cash crop, yielding the raw materials needed for the production of canvas, clothing, and rope. The colonists, including George Washington, grew marijuana.[2] Of course, they did not call it that. They called it "hemp," just as they did not call their Negro slaves "three-fifths Persons."[3] Even though many educated people no longer realize that the Constitution so stamps some of the people who built our country, at least those who do realize it understand how such fictitiously-fractional persons became real full-fledged human beings. But how many people know that hemp, coca, and the opium poppy are ordinary plants, understand how they became transformed into dreaded "dangerous drugs," and realize that, in losing our rights to them, we have *surrendered* some of our most basic rights to property?

Casting a ballot is an important act, emblematic of our role as citizens. But eating and drinking are much more important acts. If given a choice between the freedom to choose what to ingest and what politician to vote for, few if any would be so foolish as to sell his or her natural birthright to consume what he or she chooses in return for the mess of pottage of being allowed to register his or her preference for a political candidate. Yet this is precisely the bargain we, the American people, have struck with our government: more useless voting rights in exchange for fewer critical personal rights. The result is that we consider the *fiction* of self-government a blessed political right, and the *reality* of self-medication an accursed medical malady. Self-medication is synonymous with devil worship.

In 1890, less than half of adult Americans had the right to vote. Since then, one class of previously ineligible persons after another has been granted the franchise. Not only blacks and women, as they deserved, but also others with questionable claims to that privilege, for example, persons unable to speak or read English (or read and write any language). During this period, every one of us—regardless of age, education, or competence—has been deprived of his right to substances the government decides to call "dangerous drugs."

Yet, ironically, most Americans labor under the mistaken belief that they now enjoy many rights previously available only to a few (partially true only for blacks and women) and remain utterly unaware of the rights they have lost. Moreover, having become used to living in a society that wages a relentless war on drugs, we have also lost the vocabulary in which to articulate and analyze properly the disastrous social consequences of our own political-economic behavior vis-à-vis drugs. Mesmerized by the mortal dangers of fictitious new diseases, such as "chemical dependency" and "substance abuse," we have become diverted from the political perils of our totalitarian-therapeutic efforts at collective self-protection. Long ago, Frederic Bastiat (1801–1850), the French political-economic thinker and pioneer free marketeer, warned against the dangers of precisely such folly. "Protection," he wrote, "concentrates at a single point the good that it does, while the harm that it inflicts is diffused over a wide area. The good is apparent to the outer eye; the harm reveals itself only to the inner eye of the mind."[4]

Precisely wherein lies our drug problem? I submit it lies mainly in the fact that most of the psychoactive drugs we want we cannot legally make, sell, or buy—much as the Russians could not legally make, sell, or buy cars, washing machines, and the other consumer goods they craved. Why can we not do these things? Because the drugs we want are *literally* illegal, their possession constituting a criminal offense—for example, heroin and marijuana; or because they are *medically* illegal, requiring a physician's prescription—for example, steroids and Valium. In short, we have tried to solve our drug problem by prohibiting the "problem" drugs, by imprisoning the persons who make, sell, or use such drugs, by defining the use of such drugs as diseases, and by coercing drug users to undergo treatment (coercion being necessary because drug users want drugs, not treatment). None of these measures has worked. Some believe that these measures have aggravated the problem. I am sure of it, because our concept of the nature of the problem is mistaken, our methods of responding to it are coercive, and the language in which we speak about it is misleading. I submit that making, selling, and using drugs are actions, choices, decisions, behaviors—not diseases. Authorities can go far in maintaining the illusion that (ab)using a drug is a disease, but an illusion it remains.

Establish Free Market to Empower the Consumer

Since the beginning of this century, through a combination of medical licensure and direct drug control legislation, the American government has assumed progressively more authority over the drug trade and our drug use. The ostensible aim of these restrictions was to protect the people from incompetent doctors and unsafe drugs. The actual result was loss of personal freedom without the gain of promised benefits. It is important to keep in mind that our elaborate machinery of drug controls rests largely on prescription drug laws, which, in turn, rest on a medical profession licensed by the state. While in *Capitalism and Freedom*, Milton Friedman does not mention drug controls, he addresses the even more sacrosanct subject of medical licensure and gives it its libertarian due. "The conclusions I shall reach," he writes, "are that liberal principles do not justify licensure even in medicine and that in practice the results of state licensure in medicine have been undesirable."[5] Regardless of their lofty motives, drug controls encourage people to expect politicians and physicians to protect them from themselves, specifically, to protect them from their own inclinations to use or misuse certain drugs. The result is state control of the drug market and an interminable war on drugs, symptoms of our having, in effect, repealed the Constitution and the Bill of

Rights.

If we focus on the ways an American who wants to use drugs now actually gains access to them, we can distinguish three broad categories:

1. *No special government controls limiting sales:* for example, coffee, aspirin, and laxatives. Produced by private entrepreneurs and distributed through the free market, the product is called "food," "beverage," or "over-the-counter drug"; the seller, "merchant"; the buyer, "customer."

2. *Government controls limiting sales:*

a) To adults: for example, alcohol and tobacco. Produced by private entrepreneurs and distributed through the free or state-licensed market, the product is called "beer," "wine," "cigarette"; the seller, "merchant"; the buyer, "customer."

b) To patients: for example, digitalis, penicillin, steroids, and Valium. The product is produced by government-regulated pharmaceutical manufacturers and distributed through state-controlled physicians' prescriptions and pharmacies. The product is called "prescription drug"; the seller, "pharmacist"; the buyer, "patient."

c) To addicts: for example, methadone. It is produced by government-regulated pharmaceutical manufacturers and distributed through special federally approved dispensers. There are no legal sellers or buyers. The product is called "drug (abuse) treatment"; the distributor, "drug (treatment) program"; the recipient, "(certified) addict."

3. *Government controls prohibiting sales to everyone:* for example, heroin and crack. Produced illegally by private entrepreneurs and distributed through the black market, the product is called "dangerous drug" or "illegal drug"; the seller, "pusher" or "trafficker"; the buyer, "addict" or "drug abuser."

As such a market-oriented perspective on drug distribution shows, we have nothing even remotely resembling a free market in drugs in the United States. Nevertheless, most people mistakenly think of prescription drugs, and even of specifically restricted drugs, such as methadone, as legal.

Because all criticisms of drug control policies are aimed at the way particular drugs are distributed, proposals for reform correspond to the categories described above. I shall summarize each posture vis-à-vis the drug control strategies of its proponent:

1. *Criminalizers* ("Do you want more crack babies?"): Keep type

3 substances in category 3; expand categories 3, 2b, and 2c; and constrict categories 1 and 2a. Drug offenders are both criminals and patients, who should be punished as well as (coercively) treated.

2. *Legalizers* ("The war on drugs cannot be won."): Remove certain type 3 substances, such as heroin, from category 3 and transfer them to category 2b or 2c (make the manufacture and sale of heretofore prohibited substances a government monopoly). Drug abusers are sick and should be (coercively) treated in government-funded programs.

3. *Free marketeers* ("Self-medication is a right."): Abolish categories 2b, 2c, and 3, and place all presently restricted substances in category 2a. Drug use is personal choice, neither crime nor illness.

I disagree with both the drug criminalizers and the drug legalizers: with the former, because I believe that the criminal law ought to be used to protect us from others, not from ourselves; with the latter, because I believe that behavior, even if it is actually or potentially injurious or self-injurious, is not a disease and that no behavior should be regulated by sanctions called "treatment."[6]

As we have seen, there are three distinct drug markets in the United States today: the legal (free) market, the medical (prescription) market, and the illegal (black) market. Because the cost of virtually all of the services we call "drug treatment" is borne by parties other than the so-called patient and because most people submit to such treatment under legal duress, there is virtually no free market at all in drug treatment. Try as we might, we cannot escape the fact that the concept of a demand for goods and services in the free market is totally different from the concept we now employ in reference to drug use and drug treatment. In the free market, a demand is what the customer wants; or as merchandising magnate Marshall Field put it: "The customer is always right." Whereas in the prescription drug market, "the doctor is always right." The physician decides what drug the patient should "demand," and that is all he can legally get. Finally, in the psychiatric drug market, "the patient is always wrong." The psychiatrist decides what drug the mental patient "needs" and compels him to consume it, by force, if necessary.

Merchants thus *advertise*—to create a demand for the goods they want to sell: Tylenol is advertised to *customers*. Physicians *prescribe*—to open a drug market otherwise closed to persons and thus make specific drugs available to them: Penicillin is prescribed to *patients*. Psychiatrists *coerce*—to force mental patients to be drugged as they, the doctors, want them to be drugged: Haldol is forcibly injected into *psychotics.*

Ironically, the foregoing generalizations, valid until recently, are no longer so. Drug manufacturers have begun to advertise prescription drugs to the public. While this practice reveals the hitherto concealed hypocrisy of prescription laws, it introduces increasingly serious distortions into the drug market. For example, tobacco, a legal product, cannot be advertised on television, but Nicorette, an "illegal" product, can be.[7] Here are some other current examples of prescription drug advertisements aimed at the public:

For Estraderm, an estrogen patch for women: "Now the change of life doesn't have to change yours."[8]

For Minitran, a transdermal form of nitroglycerin: "Everything you asked for in a patch … for less."[9]

For Seldane, an antihistamine: "You've tried just about everything for your hay fever…. Have you tried your doctor?"[10]

And now comes the best, because the other ads are at least for diseases. But now there is an ad for a non-disease.

For Rogaine, an anti-baldness drug: "The earlier you use Rogaine, the better your chances of growing hair."[11]

The advertisement for Rogaine goes beyond simply alerting the customer to the availability of a prescription drug he might not be aware of. It offers him cash for going to see a doctor and demanding the drug. In a coupon at the bottom of the page, a smaller caption tells the reader: "Fill this in now. Then, start to fill in your hair loss." The coupon is worth ten dollars "as an incentive" to see a doctor. Because many of the prescription drugs advertised to the public are very expensive, the logic of this practice suggests that drug companies may be tempted to offer increasingly larger sums to would-be patients, in effect to bribe them to solicit a prescription from their physician.

Naturally, drug companies defend the practice. "The ads," they say, "help educate patients and give consumers a chance to become more involved in choosing the medication they want."[12] But that laudable goal could be better served by a free market in drugs. In my opinion, the practice of advertising prescription drugs to the public fulfills a more odious function, namely, to further infantilize the layperson and, at the same time, undermine the physician's medical authority. The policy puts physicians in an obvious bind. Prescription laws give doctors monopolistic privilege to provide certain drugs to certain persons or to withhold such drugs from them. Advertising prescription drugs encourages people to pressure their physicians to prescribe the drugs they *want*, rather than the drugs the physicians believe they *need*. If the doctor does not comply, the patient is likely to take his or her business elsewhere. A professor of medicine at Columbia University told *Time:* "There is no question that certain physicians are being influenced to issue prescriptions that they would not otherwise write."[13] Missing is any recognition of the way this practice reinforces the role of the patient as a helpless child and of the doctor as a providing-withholding parent.

The So-Called Drug Problem

In conclusion, I would like to mention something everyone knows, but many people often forget. Namely, the complex set of personal behaviors and social transactions we call "the drug problem" do not, in the literal sense, constitute a problem susceptible to a solution. It is a grievous mistake to conceptualize certain drugs as a "dangerous enemy" we must *attack* and *eliminate*, instead of *accepting* them as potentially helpful as well as harmful substances and learning to *cope* with them competently.

If we are to cope competently with drugs, we must accept the human desire for drugs as natural and, in principle, morally neutral. We must calmly examine the question, Why do we want drugs? In general, we want drugs for the same reasons we want other goods. Specifically, we want psychoactive drugs to relieve our pains, cure our diseases, enhance our endurance, change our moods, put us to sleep, or simply make us feel better—much as we want bicycles and cars, trucks and tractors, ladders and chain saws, skis and hang gliders to make our lives more productive and more pleasant. Each year, tens of thousands of people are injured and killed as a result of accidents associated with the use of such artifacts. Why do we not speak of "ski abuse" or a "chain saw problem?" Because we expect people who employ such equipment to familiarize themselves with their proper use and avoid injuring themselves and others. If they hurt themselves, we assume they did so accidentally and we try to help them. If they hurt others negligently, we punish them by both civil and criminal sanctions. These, in brief, are the means by which we try to *adapt* to, rather than try to *solve*, the problems presented by potentially dangerous devices in our environment.

However, after generations of living under medical tutelage, which provides us with protection (albeit illusory) against "dangerous drugs," we have failed to cultivate the self-reliance and self-discipline we must possess as competent adults surrounded by the fruits of our pharmacological-technological age. Our medical-statist drug policies thus closely resemble the Soviets Union's economic-statist policies with respect to consumer goods. After a protracted war on self-medication, we are thus mired in a mess that is its direct result, just as after a protracted war on private property, the people in the Soviet Union were mired in a mess that was its direct result.

In short, unlike most criticisms of the war on drugs, which are based on pharmacological, prudential, or therapeutic arguments, mine are based on political-philosophical considerations. I maintain that the right to chew or smoke a plant that grows wild in nature, such as hemp (marijuana), is anterior to, and more basic than, the right to vote. A limited government, such as that of the United States, lacks the political legitimacy to deprive competent adults of the right to use whatever substances they choose. The constraints on the power of the federal government, laid down in the Constitution, have been eroded by a monopolistic medical profession that administers a system of prescription laws, which have, in effect, removed most of the drugs people want from the free market. Hence, it is futile to debate whether the war on drugs should be escalated or de-escalated, without first coming to grips with the popular, medical, and political mindset concerning the trade in drugs generated by nearly a century of drug prohibitions.

The result of our protracted drug protectionist policy is that we find it impossible to legalize private property, that is, because we lack both the popular will for it and the requisite legal-political infrastructure to support it. The Soviets long ago decided that it is morally wrong to treat money (especially foreign currency) as a commodity. We long ago decided that it is morally wrong to treat drugs (especially foreign, plant-derived drugs) as a commodity. If we are satisfied with that state of affairs and its consequences, so be it.

I believe we ought to consider the possibility that a free market in drugs is not only imaginable in principle, but, given the necessary personal motivation of a people, is just as practical and beneficial as is a free market in other goods. Accordingly, I support a free market in drugs not because I think it is, at this moment, a practical policy, but because I believe it is right and because, in the long run, I believe the right policy may also be the practical policy.

Notes

[1] *Stanley v. Georgia,* 394 U.S. 557 (1969); *Roe v. Wade,* 410 U.S. 113 (1973).

[2] J.F. Hopkins, *A History of the Hemp Industry in Kentucky* (Lexington: University of Lexington Press, 1951); B. Moore, *A Study of the Past, the Present and the Possibilities of the Hemp Industry in Kentucky* (Lexington: James E. Hughes, 1905), and G. Washington, "Diary Notes," cited in L. Grinspoon, *Marihuana Reconsidered,* 2d ed. (Cambridge: Harvard University Press, 1977), pp. 10–12.

[3] Constitution of the United States, Article I, Section 2.

[4] F. Bastiat, *Economic Sophisms* (1845/1848), trans. by Arthur Goddard (Princeton: Van Nostrand, 1964), p. 4.

[5] M. Friedman, *Capitalism and Freedom* (Chicago: University of Chicago Press, 1962), p. 138. *See also* Chapter 3, "Medical Licensure," p. 15.

[6] Although it is a truism, it is perhaps necessary to repeat that the uncorrupted concept of liberty implies no particular result, only the proverbial level playing field where all can play—and win or lose—by the same rules. Despite the rhetoric to the contrary, no one is, or can be, killed by an illegal drug. If a person dies as a result of using a drug, it is because he chose to do something risky: the drug he chooses may be cocaine or Cytoxan; the risk he chooses to incur may be motivated by the pressure of peers or the pressure of cancer. In either case, the drug may kill him. Some deaths attributed to illegal drug use may thus be accidents (for example, inadvertent overdose); some may be indirect suicides (playing Russian roulette with unknown drugs); and some may be direct suicides (deliberate overdose).

[7] Nicorette is a nicotine-containing chewing gum.

[8] *Lear's,* March 1990.

[9] *TV Guide,* May 19–25, 1990.

[10] *People,* May 21, 1990.

[11] *Time,* Dec. 17, 1990, p. 19.

[12] A. Purvis, "Just What the Patient Ordered," *Time,* May 28, 1990, p. 42.

[13] Ibid.

Chapter Seventeen

Iconoclastic Psychiatrist

*T**his chapter is adapted from an interview on "America's Drug Forum," a national public affairs talk show that appears on public television stations. Randy Paige is an Emmy Award-winning drug reporter from Baltimore, Maryland.*

PAIGE: What do you mean by the title, *Our Right to Drugs?*

SZASZ: I mean by that that the government of the United States, as it was constituted by the Founding Fathers and as it continues to operate, more or less, does not have the political legitimacy to tell us what we ingest, what we drink or eat. Just like it cannot tell us what food to put into our mouths, it doesn't have the legitimacy to control what we take in. And therefore, I don't distinguish between drugs and food in this respect. It does not have the right to protect us from ourselves.

PAIGE: What about the business of drugs, the business of illegal drugs? Does the government have a right to tell somebody you can't sell drugs to that person?

SZASZ: Well, I believe in a free market in drugs; therefore, that would be similar to the government prohibiting you from selling tomatoes on a roadside or corn. So, that's not the part of the government's business. That is, I view drug prohibition as illegal governmental activity, just as if it prohibited Catholicism or Judaism. It's not for the government to decide what religion to permit.

That's why, although this may sound pedantic, I strongly oppose the term *legalize,* because *legalize* implies that the government gives us a permission to do these things, but that's not what the Founding Fathers said. They don't give us rights, the rights are inalienable. They can only take away rights. So, that's what I mean by "our right to drugs."

The show upon which this chapter is based is entitled "Thomas Szasz: Maverick Psychiatrist," no. 224 (1991).

PAIGE: How would you respond to critics who would suggest that the government has the right, for example, to refuse providing an automatic weapon to a man who's known to commit violence?

SZASZ: Well, I would very quickly want to dissociate that kind of a metaphor because a weapon's primary purpose is to injure someone.

PAIGE: Do you believe the government has a right to restrict an individual for any reason? Are there any reasons that are good enough for a government to say, "You can't do that?"

SZASZ: Well, of course, it does. I'm not an anarchist.

PAIGE: OK.

SZASZ: In fact, the government doesn't have a *right*, the government has a *duty* to punish you or me if we deprive another person of life, liberty, or property. It doesn't have that right; it has that duty. It has fallen down on that duty because it's doing something else.

PAIGE: OK. Then for argument's sake, what about the drug dealer who goes up to a ten-year old...

SZASZ: There is no drug dealer. There is no drug dealer.

PAIGE: OK.

SZASZ: We don't talk about sugar dealers or cucumber dealers. There are no drug dealers, there are people who sell drugs.

PAIGE: OK. So, the person who sells drugs, let's say, to a young child. There are those who would argue that that person is affecting that other innocent person.

SZASZ: Hold it. I have made an assumption, which I hope people who listen to a serious show like this would also make. And I don't blame you for bringing in the conventional rhetoric.

PAIGE: Devil's advocate. Right.

SZASZ: Kids. Merrill Lynch can't sell stocks and bonds to children. A real estate agent can't sell houses to children. We are not talking about children. Children do not have any rights. They don't have a right to freedom of religion; they have to follow their parents. We are talking about adults. So, I'm not talking about children. Children ought to be controlled, first of all, by their parents and, secondly, possibly by some delegated authorities of the state. We are talking about adults only.

PAIGE: So, how would you like to see the United States deal generally first—and then we'll get more specific—generally with the problem of drug use, the areas in drug use which are affecting people adversely?

SZASZ: You've got my thinking and who I am a little bit wrong, because when you say, how would I like the United States to deal with it, it implies that I am the sort of person who somehow would like to have some political power and tell people how to deal with this. I view myself, in this respect, more like a historian who looks back at what people did fifty years ago, except I am sort of looking at what people are doing now. And what I see is that the American people are scared to death of the freedom to have a free market in drugs. Now if they are scared of this, who am I to tell them that they should have it? Just like the Iranians are scared to death of a free market in religion.

PAIGE: Where does that fear come from?

SZASZ: It comes from a one-hundred-year war on drugs, whose foundation is the prescription market; not the illegal [market], not heroin. People are afraid of penicillin, of digitalis. That's what they are afraid of. They think they have to go to a doctor to get these drugs without informing themselves. You can be a professor of pharmacology at the local medical school and know more about drugs than nine out of ten physicians. But if your daughter has a sore throat, a strep throat, that professor of pharmacology cannot legally buy any penicillin. That is what I am talking about.

PAIGE: I see.

SZASZ: And there is no interest even in discussing this. When people talk about a drug conference, they always talk about marijuana, but marijuana's not even a drug; it's a plant.

PAIGE: But there are those who would suggest that there are chemicals in that plant that affect you as a drug would affect you.

SZASZ: Well, there are chemicals in every plant. There are chemicals in everything.

PAIGE: What is the biggest mistake in the basic moral tenets which support the nation's war on drugs?

SZASZ: Again, I would like to turn it around. I think people like to persecute other people. My feeling about the history of the world is that it is a history of persecutions. The only question is: Who do we persecute? And it is particularly striking in this country. Now I am very happy to be in this country. I wasn't born in this country. I'm grateful for it. But I am well aware of the fact that this country was united for a long time by the hatred of blacks, called slavery. Then there was another back-up of persecuted groups, women, who after all didn't get the vote until sixty years after the blacks got it. Now, weren't they persons?

I came to this country in 1938, and what happened three years later? Warren Burger, Franklin Roosevelt, the American Civil Liberties Union all decided that a three-year-old boy born in Los Angeles, whose grandparents lived in Sacramento, is a mortal danger to the U.S. So, he's going to be put in a concentration camp. I wasn't. People from Germany weren't. But the Japanese who lived here were enemy aliens. Do you know what I call this? Scapegoating. Scapegoating is the metabolism of society.

PAIGE: So, how does the present drug policy fit into that?

SZASZ: In my view, we have, what I called twenty-five years ago, a Therapeutic State. The imagery in our country is that the most important value is health. And in the name of health it is OK to lock up people, to beat people, to deprive them of their constitutional rights, and even to kill them.

And, this is led by physicians, psychiatrists, and politicians. And if you look at the writings and the speeches of someone like William Bennett, you see a scapegoater. He actually said people should be decapitated. There was no outcry about this. Nobody said this is a metaphor. Nancy Reagan became famous for saying there can be not enough intolerance towards drugs. Intolerance towards anyone is, in my book, a sin. You can hate someone who does criminal acts, but, in principle, to be intolerant towards a group of people seems to me to be an inelegant idea.

Now this is just the tip of the iceberg. How many red-blooded American parents think that the best thing they can do for their nineteen-year-old son, if he smokes marijuana, is to denounce him to the police? This is Nazism. This is communism. We have, in effect, a kind of state chemical fascism, in which denouncing people to the police, to the government—children denouncing parents and parents denouncing children—are the cardinal immoralities. Now this was done by the Reagans, who kept saying, "Talk about family values." What's more important, the family or the state?

PAIGE: So, you would say that the war on drugs is morally bankrupt.

SZASZ: No, it's morally flourishing.

PAIGE: Forgive me. But what I mean by that is the moral foundations for it are bankrupt.

SZASZ: No. What I am saying is that I repudiate its moral foundations, but that ninety-nine percent of the American people and one hundred percent of the American political system, Congress, the Supreme Court, the American Medical Association, the American Bar Association—I could go on and on—they all support it. Who is against it?

I go further than that. During Prohibition, there were people like H. L. Mencken; there were humorists. What prominent person, writer, artist is now against the war on drugs and says the government does not have the right to deprive you of marijuana, otherwise called hemp, any more than it does of mushrooms or dandelions? It's like drinking dandelion tea. It's growing wild on the highways. You pick it you, you put it in your pocket, you're a criminal. This is not America.

I should mention what people don't know: so-called drug education is a huge lie. What people don't know is, that between 1776 and 1914, all drugs were completely legal. Now drugs haven't changed, human physiology hasn't changed, and the Constitution has not been changed with respect to drugs. So, where does the right come from to deprive us of these drugs?

With alcohol at least there was a decency to write a constitutional amendment to make it illegal. OK. But there is no constitutional amendment with respect to penicillin.

PAIGE: I have heard some enforcers suggest that the United States made a big mistake with alcohol. That the big mistake was made when there was a conscious decision not only to make it available in a free market, but to allow alcohol to become glorified in movies, in advertising, to become a part of the social fabric. And that, because of that, a lot of misery in this country has resulted and that, therefore, there is a need to restrict drugs. Your response?

SZASZ: This country made a much bigger mistake. It opted for freedom. Freedom means the opportunity to not take care of yourself properly.

PAIGE: But you don't see that as a mistake ?

SZASZ: I call that the Fall of Man. That's already in the Bible. If you have the right to choose things, you have the option to choose well and to choose badly—otherwise known as the stock market. So, there is a joke: What kind of stock should I buy? The kind that goes up.

PAIGE: Is there a parallel between what you have seen in your study of the growth of psychiatry and what you have also seen in terms of the nation's drug policy?

SZASZ: Well, my view of psychiatry, as it relates to the drug policy, very briefly, is as follows. I divide psychiatry into two entirely separate categories and enterprises in a way which is not conventional, but very easily understood. I distinguish between consenting adults, voluntary—you go to a therapist and, if you don't like it, you leave. And then there is a psychiatry which consists really of a prison operation where you get locked up, exemplified by John Hinckley being ostensibly in a mental hospital a few blocks from here. Well, I don't call that a hospital, I call that a prison because he can't leave.

Now I see coercive psychiatry, which is a core of psychiatry—psychiatric impositions of unwanted diagnoses, unwanted treatment, unwanted hospitalization—as the handmaiden of the war on drugs. Because people talk about "criminalization" and "medicalization." Now I call that a rose by any other name. You can lock up someone in a prison and you can lock up somebody in a mental hospital. Now if you lock up somebody in a mental hospital, you create the illusion that somehow you are more humane, that you are doing some therapy. I personally think medicalization is worse than criminalization because it looks better and, therefore, is more deceptive.

PAIGE: But you think that a lot of the same elements are at play.

SZASZ: Not a lot. All of the same elements are in play, of which there is only one element, because I only recognize one variable here, and that's coercion. The state either leaves you alone or doesn't leave you alone. Now if it doesn't leave you alone, it doesn't matter whether it's doctors in white coats or policemen in blue coats who come after you.

PAIGE: How about the intentions? Do you believe the people who are instrumenting this nation's drug policy, such a President George Bush and former drug czar William Bennett and others, have noble intentions but are misguided, or do you believe that they are intentionally trying to coerce the American public?

SZASZ: Not quite either. Let me say this. I do not, in principle, without mentioning these particular persons, believe in politicians with noble intentions. I am sort of like Mark Twain. He said that there is only one native criminal class in America, that's Congress. That may be a little strong, but just a little. I think they are just as self-serving as anyone else, except a little bit more so probably because they have their hands on the government coercive apparatus. So, suspending the issue of their particular motives, I do not have any doubt that they have their ears tuned to what the American public wants. And what the American public wants is what every public has wanted since the Romans: bread and circuses. And the circuses means that, in the name of something good, you meddle, bother, and persecute people who have been defined as enemies of the state. The crack dealer in Harlem.

PAIGE: Sounds pretty ominous.

SZASZ: Sounds pretty ominous. Who can be for the "crack dealer in Harlem"? Who can be for the "usurious Jews," the "Christ killer"? The "yellow-bellied Jap"? The "Kraut"? "The only good Indian is a dead Indian?" And one can go on and on.

PAIGE: Let me ask you the same question, but turn it around. What about the case of the sixty-five or seventy-five-year-old man or woman who lives on a corner in Harlem, who look out on their street corner every morning and they see armed young men selling drugs and they're afraid to go out, and they're afraid to have their grandchildren come and visit them? Do they have right to have some other kinds of expectations?

SZASZ: Well, I'm afraid that that question really doesn't belong—to be addressed to me because that is a product of what George Bush and Nancy Reagan and Jimmy Carter and so on have brought about.

PAIGE: In what way?

SZASZ: Well, there wouldn't be this commotion at the corner of Harlem if you could sell cocaine like you sell powdered sugar. There's no war about selling sugar or green peppers in Harlem. If you don't mind my being so strong, you are confusing the effect of the war on drugs with the effect of the existence of drugs. Drugs are inert substances.

How come there were no drug wars before 1914? You could buy all the heroin from Sears, Roebuck in 1913 through a catalog, but how come there were no drug wars? You answer it.

If you talk to someone who used to use drugs and no longer is using drugs, you often will find someone who is a staunch supporter of drug enforcement. Former addicts or recovering addicts have told me that the reason they didn't get further down the road of drug use was because it was so expensive and because they had so much to lose by continuing that activity.

Take a drug such as crack cocaine, which is extremely—talk to people who use it—extremely difficult to stop using once you start, and make it readily available, as sugar or any commodity is available in any store with no restrictions. With restrictions to children.

PAIGE: OK. But other than that, no restrictions.

SZASZ: Of course.

PAIGE: Wouldn't you have a tremendous increase in the number of people whose lives have been devastated by drug use?

SZASZ: Excuse me. You are a native speaker of English and your business is to interview people, but the language in which you package this I find objectionable, because there would be no lives wasted. People will have wasted their lives. Lives don't get wasted. I believe in free will. And what you are pointing out is that if people would have more options in life, then some of them may use them unwisely.

There are only two ways of controlling human behavior: with self-discipline and with external coercion. I believe in a society in which most people control themselves and the least number of people are controlled externally, which means by the police. Most people, especially people who get used to misusing themselves, so-called addicts, feel that they don't have enough controls and they want someone else to control them, whether it's Ayatollah Khomeini or the U.S. Marine Corps. People love to submit themselves to authorities and then usually complain later on of what the authorities did to them.

PAIGE: What about those who are not willing participants, such as babies who are born addicted or pregnant women?

SZASZ: Well, that's an entirely different and very complicated subject. How about babies who are born diabetic, because both parents are diabetics? It's much better to be healthy than to be sick. And the fact that so many parents, adults, abuse their right to procreate is still another subject. Perhaps we should look more closely at the right to procreate, which directly affects society and other people, rather than the right of a fifty-year-old businessman to smoke a marijuana cigarette instead of a tobacco cigarette.

Procreation is a very complicated issue. We certainly can't get into that. But children do get damaged or are brought into the world damaged for reasons other than the drug problem. Again, this is a selective indignation.

PAIGE: Look down the road five years from now. Assuming that the system you would like to see in place—that is, that drugs would be legal for those who are…

SZASZ: No, no, you are putting words in my mouth.

PAIGE: Forgive me.

SZASZ: I don't think that system can be in place any more than a real capitalist system can be in place in Russia five years from now.

PAIGE: So, you're saying, realistically, it's never going to happen.

SZASZ: Not never.

PAIGE: OK. But not in five years.

SZASZ: But not in five years.

PAIGE: I guess what I meant was if by some strange wave of the hand you could magically transform this country into that system, what would you see? Once that system were in place, what kind of a world would you see? How would it be better than it is today?

SZASZ: Well, it would be better, first of all, that the government coercive apparatus—in other words, the police, the judiciary—would presumably be [paying] more attention to making it possible for you and me to go out and take a walk around in Washington, D.C., see these nice things lit up at eleven o'clock at night, as we could when I came to this country in 1938. We could go to New York and go to a theater on 46th Street, maybe we could go back to the Hilton without a taxi or without being scared lest we are mugged. In other words, the government would return to us our right to be protected on our streets and in our homes from criminals. Number one.

Number two. There would be a lot of productive activity, which is now used unproductively in prosecuting the so-called war on drugs. Arresting people who are innocent of any wrongdoing: growers, users, police, and so on. Again, this whole apparatus.

Thirdly, morally the fabric of the country would be improved because the subtle, unsaid message would be: You have wonderful opportunities in this country if you control yourself. And if you don't control yourself, then you make yourself sick and we will do nothing to stop it. If you want to drink yourself to death, good luck to you. If you want to smoke yourself to death, get lung cancer, and we will not pay for it. And I think that would be a decent society.

People who do well would reap the consequences of that, just as if you are a good parent and are nice to your children, then you have the pleasure of having nice children from the age of twenty until you die. If you are a bad parent, then you have children which you wish had never lived. And that's the way it should be.

PAIGE: Do you believe that those who have been born in this country and belong to families who've been here for many generations take less for granted the things that this country originally stood for? Do you think that your vantage point as an immigrant enables you to see this problem in a unique way or a more realistic way?

SZASZ: I have thought of that and my answer would be probably not, because again I am rather realistic or pessimistic. After all, I know lots of people who have the same immigrant experience and who are arch-coercers. In fact, a great many immigrant psychiatrists believe that everybody is mentally ill and should be locked up, given electric shock, lobotomy, all against their will. They are the most statist—if you like fascist—[they] have the most fascist mentality.

I don't think there's any one group, immigrant, non-immigrants, blacks, whites, men, women, I think they all behave more or less similarly. Freedom is one of those scary concepts. We all want it when we lose it. When you have AIDS, then you want a particular drug which the government prevents, but not the others. When you're a woman, then you want some birth control device that the government doesn't want you to have that you can get in France. But again, that same feminist group doesn't want you to have heroin. When you are dying, you're ninety years old and dying of metastatic cancer, then you say, "Why can't I have heroin in America?" Well, why shouldn't you have heroin even when you're thirty?

PAIGE: Does the present drug policy make you angry?

SZASZ: Absolutely not. I see the present drug policy as a kind of Nazism with which one can live. It's a democratic Nazi, but it doesn't pick on Jews, it picks on everybody.

PAIGE: But it doesn't make…

SZASZ: No, actually, it doesn't pick on everybody. I see it essentially as a war on blacks.

PAIGE: In what way?

SZASZ: Most of the victims of the war on drugs are blacks. If you look at an average television show of a drug bust, everybody looks black or Hispanic. If you look in a jail where the drug addicts are, most of them look black. One statistic says that there are more blacks in prison for drug offenses in the U.S. than there are blacks in colleges. Under my system, none of them would be in prison.

So, when you say how will it be better? This is a message which already someone else, in part, has picked up, and I am convinced that this is, in part, why he was assassinated. Malcolm X said that the drug problem is a problem of American whites waging a drug war so

American blacks would become addicted and can use drugs.

PAIGE: I have heard it said that a black man with a Malcolm X book in his back pocket is far more dangerous than a black man with a crack pipe in his back pocket. Would you agree?

SZASZ: Because nothing is more dangerous to a government than an independently thinking person. He is the real danger because he doesn't need the government and he knows that the government is a storehouse of lies. We talk about "drug education." That's an oxymoron. It's like Army intelligence, you know, a classic joke.

PAIGE: So, where do we go from here?

SZASZ: That depends on the American people, just like it depended on the Russian people, on the German people. Didn't the Germans like persecuting Jews? Didn't the Russians like persecuting people because they had hard currency in their pockets? Look at even the language: hard currency, hard drugs. What's so bad about having foreign currency in your pocket? You were shot for that until very recently, for seventy years. Did the Russian people rise up against it? No, they loved it.

PAIGE: Will it change?

SZASZ: I think the American war on drugs will only change when a majority of the American people will be injured by it *directly* through withholding of essential drugs, especially when they are very sick, when they are in pain. This is already happening. If you have some dreadfully painful disease and are in a hospital, the chances are that your treatment will be greatly inferior to what it would have been a hundred years ago. There is no other medical condition for which you can make that statement. Because a hundred years ago you would have gotten adequate analgesics. You could have bought it on the street without a doctor.

Now we hear about pain clinics, pain control studies. You know what I call pain clinics? Doctors who *withhold* pain medication—they are called pain researchers.

PAIGE: It sounds diabolical.

SZASZ: No more than human nature. Human nature consists of doing dirt to other people; except for Jefferson and Madison, who said let's make the government weak. Because throughout human history, few people have done a lot of dirt to a lot of other people. That's why people like to come to this country. Because it's least bad here.

PAIGE: So are you not optimistic then for the future?

Szasz: For the drug war? I'm neither optimistic nor pessimistic. I think when enough people will get injured by it, then it will change. Until then, it won't change.

Paige: Why do you believe that you are in such a minority in your assessment?

Szasz: For the same reason when, during the so-called McCarthy days, the Bill of Rights was circularized—somebody did this experiment of distributing or showing people a copy of the Bill of Rights on the streets of Minneapolis and Detroit and so on—and ninety-eight out of one hundred people said, "This is a communist document, subversive to American values. Who did this? He should be locked up. He should be executed."

Paige: If there's one thought that you would want to leave our viewers with—people in South Dakota and California, Colorado, Florida—what would that be?

Szasz: Go back to the principle of self-discipline and to the Mark Twainian principle that the business of official authorities—doctors, lawyers, teachers, the government—who have power is to lie. Because if you want to tell the truth, then you don't need any power. Anyone who seizes power is ipso facto a liar. Back to Socrates. And what happened to Socrates?

Additional Readings

On Liberty and Drugs:

Bakalar, James B. and Lester Grinspoon. *Drug Control in a Free Society*. Cambridge, England: Cambridge University Press, 1984.

Barnett, Randy E. *The Rights Retained by the People: The History and Meaning of the Ninth Amendment*. Fairfax, VA: George Mason University Press, 1989.

Bastiat, Frederic. *Economic Sophisms*. Princeton: Van Nostrand, 1964.

Boaz, David, ed. *The Crisis in Drug Prohibition*. Washington, D.C.: Cato Institute, 1990.

Evans, Rod L. and Irwin M. Berent. *Drug Legalization: For and Against*. LaSalle, IL: Open Court Publishing Co., 1992.

Glasser, Ira. *Visions of Liberty: The Bill of Rights for all Americans*. New York: Little, Brown & Company, 1991.

Hamowy, Ronald, ed. *Dealing with Drugs: Consequences of Government Control*. Lexington, MA: Lexington Books, 1987.

Hayek, Friedrich A. *The Road to Serfdom*. Chicago: The Chicago University Press, 1944, 1972.

———. *The Fatal Conceit: The Errors of Socialism*. W.W. Bartley III, ed. Chicago: The University of Chicago Press, 1989.

Hazlitt, Henry. *Economics in One Lesson*. Westport, CT: Arlington House, 1946, 1962, 1979.

King, Rufus. *The Drug Hang-Up: America's Fifty-Year Folly*. Springfield, IL: Charles C. Thomas, Publisher, 1974.

Macedo, Stephen. *The New Right v. the Constitution*. Washington, D.C.: Cato Institute, 1987.

Machan, Tibor R., ed. *The Libertarian Alternative: Essays in Social and Political Philosophy*. Chicago: Nelson-Hall, 1974.

Mackay, Charles. *Extraordinary Popular Delusions and the Madness of Crowds* [1841, 1852]. New York: Harmony Books, 1980.

Maddox, William S. and Stuart A. Lilie. *Beyond Liberal and Conservative: Reassessing the Political Spectrum*. Washington, D.C.: Cato Institute, 1984.

Mill, John Stuart. *On Liberty* (1859).

Mises, Ludwig von. *Socialism: An Economic and Sociological Analysis.* 1922. Reprint. Trans. from the 2d German ed. (1932) by J. Kahane. Indianapolis: Liberty Classics, 1981.

———. *Human Action: A Treatise on Economics.* New Haven: Yale University Press, 1949.

Peele, Stanton. *Diseasing of America: Addiction Treatment out of Control.* Lexington, MA: Lexington Books, 1989.

Richards, David A.J. *Sex, Drugs, Death, and the Law: An Essay on Human Rights and Overcriminalization.* Totowa, NJ: Rowman and Littlefield, 1982.

Smith, Adam. *The Wealth of Nations* (1776).

Thornton, Mark. *The Economics of Prohibition.* Salt Lake City: University of Utah Press, 1991.

Trebach, Arnold S. *The Heroin Solution.* New Haven: Yale University Press, 1982.

———. *The Great Drug War.* New York: Macmillan Publishing Co. and Washington, D.C.: The Drug Policy Foundation Press, 1987.

——— and James A. Inciardi. *Legalize It? Debating American Drug Policy.* Washington, D.C.: American University Press, 1993.

Wisotsky, Steven. *Beyond the War on Drugs: Overcoming a Failed Public Policy.* Buffalo, NY: Prometheus Books, 1990.

Other Books by Milton Friedman:

Capitalism and Freedom. Chicago: The University of Chicago Press, 1962, 1982.

A Monetary History of the United States, 1867–1960, with Anna J. Schwartz. Princeton: Princeton University Press, 1963.

An Economist's Protest. Glen Ridge, NJ: Thomas Horton and Company, 1972, 1975. Also published as *There's No Such Thing as a Free Lunch.* LaSalle, IL: Open Court Publishing Co., 1975.

Bright Promises, Dismal Performance. San Diego: Harcourt Brace Jovanovich, 1983.

Other Books by Milton and Rose D. Friedman:

Free to Choose: A Personal Statement. San Diego: Harcourt Brace Jovanovich, 1979, 1980, 1990.

Tyranny of the Status Quo. San Diego: Harcourt Brace Jovanovich, 1984.

Other Books by Thomas S. Szasz:

The Myth of Mental Illness: Foundations of a Theory of Personal Conduct. Revised edition. New York: Perennial Library, 1974. (Originally published in 1961.)

Law, Liberty, and Psychiatry: An Inquiry into the Social Uses of Mental Health Practices. Syracuse, NY: Syracuse University Press, 1963, 1989.

Ideology and Insanity: Essays on the Psychiatric Dehumanization of Man. Syracuse, NY: Syracuse University Press, 1970, 1991.

The Manufacture of Madness: A Comparative Study of the Inquisition and the Mental Health Movement. New York: Harper & Row, 1970.

Ceremonial Chemistry: The Ritual Persecution of Drugs, Addicts, and Pushers. Revised edition. Holmes Beach, FL: Learning Publications, Inc., 1985. (Originally published in 1974.)

The Theology of Medicine: The Political-Philosophical Foundation of Medical Ethics. Syracuse, NY: Syracuse University Press, 1977, 1988.

The Myth of Psychotherapy: Mental Healing as Religion, Rhetoric, and Repression. Syracuse, NY: Syracuse University Press, 1978, 1988.

Sex by Prescription: The Startling Truth about Today's Sex Therapy. Syracuse, NY: Syracuse University Press, 1980, 1990.

The Therapeutic State: Psychiatry in the Mirror of Current Events. Buffalo, NY: Prometheus Books, 1984.

The Untamed Tongue: A Dissenting Dictionary. LaSalle, IL: Open Court Publishing Co., 1990.

Our Right to Drugs: The Case for a Free Market. New York: Praeger Publishers, 1992.

Other Books Published by the Drug Policy Foundation:

Trebach, Arnold S. and Kevin B. Zeese, eds. *Drug Policy 1989–1990: A Reformer's Catalogue* (1989).

———. *Drug Prohibition and the Conscience of Nations* (1990).

———. *The Great Issues of Drug Policy* (1990).

———. *New Frontiers in Drug Policy* (1991).

———. *Strategies for Change* (1992).

Index

About the Authors

PROFESSOR MILTON FRIEDMAN has been a Senior Research Fellow at the Hoover Institution on War, Revolution, and Peace at Stanford since 1977. He is also Paul Snowden Russell Distinguished Service Professor Emeritus of Economics at the University of Chicago, where he taught from 1946 to 1976.

Friedman received his B.A. in 1932 from Rutgers University, an A.M. in 1933 from the University of Chicago, and a Ph.D. in 1946 from Columbia University.

Friedman is considered the leader of the Chicago School of monetary economics, which stresses the importance of the quantity of money in government policies and in business cycles and inflation. For his work on monetary economics, Professor Friedman won the Nobel Memorial Prize in Economic Science in 1976. He is also the recipient of the National Medal of Science and the Presidential Medal of Freedom by the U.S. government in 1988. In 1991, the Drug Policy Foundation awarded Friedman its top honor, the Richard J. Dennis Drugpeace Award for Outstanding Achievement in the Field of Drug Policy Reform.

DR. THOMAS S. SZASZ has taught psychiatry at the State University of New York Health Science Center in Syracuse since 1956, and he is currently Professor of Psychiatry Emeritus there. Szasz is also an adjunct scholar at the Cato Institute in Washington, D.C.

Szasz earned his A.B. with Honors in Physics in 1941 and his M.D. in 1944 from the University of Cincinnati. He then received his Diplomate from the National Board of Medical Examiners in 1945, his Diploma from the Chicago Institute for Psychoanalysis in 1950, and his Diplomate in Psychiatry from the American Board of Psychiatry and Neurology in 1951.

Szasz has been honored for his commitment to individual liberty in numerous ways. The American Humanist Association named him Humanist of the Year for 1974. He received the Mencken Award from the Free Press Association in 1981. In 1990, the Center for Independent Thought established The Thomas S. Szasz Award for Outstanding Contributions to the Cause of Civil Liberties. The Drug Policy Foundation presented Dr. Szasz with the 1991 Alfred R. Lindesmith Award for Achievement in the Field of Scholarship and Writing.